Octo

Fifty

Four

Joe Curtis

First Edition 2021

First Return Press
11 Park Avenue
Dublin 16
Ireland

Sold by Amazon

ISBN: 9798727117842

Contents

General
Politics   5
Religion   10

Dublin
Domestic Life   26
Shopping   37
Entertainment   54
Sport   77
Radio   84
Newspapers   93
Transport   98
Education   113
Employment   118
Health   140
Peace & Justice   146

Rural Ireland   150

World Affairs   165

Introduction

Some wise owl said that "you can only know where you are going, if you know where you came from". In my case, I have arrived, unaided by this piece of wisdom, and now I am simply curious about the land of my birth.

I was born in Dublin in October 1954, just a few decades after the Irish War of Independence, and a few short years after the end of the Second World War, although Ireland was substantially a neutral country during the latter monstrous event.

This book explores the era of my birth, and tries to re-capture what Dublin looked like in the month of my birth, and by implication, the year of my birth, whilst also capturing some glimpses of the rest of Ireland, and indeed the world in general.

The various newspapers of 1954 have been heavily relied upon for much of the information in this book.

Symbols

Prices are listed in "pounds (£), shillings (s) and pennies (d)", for example, £2.5.6d. There were twenty shillings in a pound, and twelve pennies in a shilling. The humble penny went a long way in 1954, especially for small boys, since it was divided into four farthings, or two halfpennies. A six-penny piece was nicknamed a "tanner", and shillings were nicknamed "bob". Pounds were nicknamed "quid". A Half Crown was 2/6 (two shillings and six pence). A florin was two shillings. A guinea was 21 shillings (£1 and 1 shilling) often quoted for important transactions or expensive goods.

Groceries were weighted in stones, pounds and ounces: 16 ounces equated with 1 pound (lb), 14 lb equated to I stone, and 8 stone equated to 1cwt (hundredweight). Four ounces equated to 1 qt (quarter), a common measurement for sweets and loose biscuits.

Items were measured in feet and inches: 12 inches equated to 1 foot; 3 feet equated to 1 yard.

Politics

General

In 1954, Ireland was still a fledgling state, following Independence from Britain in 1922, and the country was ravaged by unemployment and emigration, partly because of the trade war with Britain, introduced by Fianna Fail in 1932. Trade barriers were not abolished until the Sean Lemass (FF) era starting in 1959. The population of the Republic was about 2.9 million and falling, until it began to rise in the 1970's. The world was still recovering from the terrible Second World War, even though it ended in 1945.

Parties

The inexperienced politicians of the 1950's were veterans of the 1916 Rising, the War of independence, and the Civil War, resulting in two rival political parties, Fine Gael which achieved Independence by signing the treaty, and Fianna Fail which preferred to be obstructive and sit on the fence. Their children carried on the 1916-1922 era traditions, thereby keeping Ireland in a rut for generations to come. As an example of the age profile of politicians, Eamon de Valera celebrated his 72nd birthday on the 14th October.

However, following an election in May, called by Eamon de Valera of Fianna Fail, neither of the two big parties had a majority, and so a coalition of Fine Gael and Labour came to power, with John Costello of Fine Gael as Taoiseach. The results were: Fianna Fail – 65, Fine Gael- 50, Labour - 19, Clan na Poblacta (Republican Party) – 3, Clan na Talmhan (Farmers Party)– 5, Independents – 5. Total 146.

On 2nd June, there was a Solemn Votive Mass in the Pro-Cathedral of Dublin, presided over by Archbishop McQuaid, to invoke God's Blessing on the new 15th Dail.

President Sean T. O'Ceallaigh (O'Kelly) occupied Arus an Uachtarain in the Phoenix Park from 1945 to 1959.

Northern Ireland

The partition of Ireland in 1920 by the departing British occupiers was still a subject for hot debate on both sides of the land bordar, with such newspaper headlines in October as "How Stormont Holds Minority in Check". Lord Brookeborough, Premier of Northern Ireland, was adamant that the Irish Tricolour flag would never be allowed to fly in the British province.

Even before the Border Campaign by the Irish Republican Army (IRA) from 1956 to 1962, there were previous episodes concerning the partition of Ireland. For example, on 19th April 1954, there was an Anti-Partition parade in Dublin from Arbour Hill to the General Post Office (GPO) in O'Connell Street, with 1,000 marchers participating. Later that same year, there were two armed raids on British Army Barracks in Northern Ireland. The first was Gough Barracks in Armagh in June, where 300 rifles and automatics were stolen in broad daylight by fifteen men dressed in British Army uniforms, and not one shot was fired. The second (unsuccessful) raid was in October at the Royal Inniskilling Fusiliers depot (barracks) in Omagh, after which eight men were caught and imprisoned for between 10 and 12 years. In November, students marched/protested in O'Connell Street, Dublin, in support of these IRA prisoners.

In August, Queen Elizabeth visited Belfast, and there were pickets mounted outside the British Embassy in Merrion Square East, Dublin.

Public Events

On the 18th April, a wreath was laid by Taoiseach Eamon de Valera at Arbour Hill Cemetery in Dublin to honour the 1916 leaders. Senator Margaret Pearse (sister of Patrick and Willie Pearse) recited a decade of the Rosary in Irish, the Irish flag was raised from half-mast, and the buglers sounded the Last Post and Reveille.

President O'Kelly unveiled the Old IRA Celtic Cross in Harold's Cross on April, honouring the 4th Battalion, Dublin Brigade, Old IRA. There was a Guard of Honour by the 26th Battalion, FCA, and the Army No 1 Band played rousing tunes. A special Mass was celebrated in the Holy Rosary Church by Fr Flood, and that evening there was a Memorial Concert in the National Stadium on the nearby South Circular Road.

In June, a bronze plaque was unveiled by outgoing Taoiseach de Valera at Rathfarnham Bridge, in honour of the Pearse Brothers, attended by a big crown of Old IRA members.

Also in June, General Sean MacEoin, Minister for Defence, laid a wreath at Bodenstown Cemetery, Co Kildare, in memory of Theobald Wolfe Tone.

In June, a big rough granite boulder with a small bas-relief plaque was unveiled by President O'Kelly in St Stephens Green, in honour of O'Donovan Rossa, with two elderly daughters from New York in attendance. The scale of the memorial and the chosen site is really an insult to most Irish people, being inferior to the nearby massive monumental archway at the north-west corner of St Stephens Green, which glorifies the imperialist British Boer War (1899/1900) in South Africa, and by implication glorifies the shocking apartheid system which was later introduced. During the Boer War, the British as usual engaged in vicious tactics, including their "Scorched-Earth" policy, and set up massive Concentration Camps, where thousands of civilians, including women and children, suffered horrible disease-ridden deaths. Of course, the British Empire, in reality a handful of greedy British industrialists, only wanted to steal the diamonds and gold deposits belonging to the African people.

In July, the signing of the 1921 Truce was celebrated, with a Mass in Holy Trinity Church, Dublin Castle. There was a small parade to Parnell Square, led by the Post Office Workers Union Band.

On the 7th November, Remembrance Sunday (remembering the two World Wars) was celebrated (by Irish Protestants) in the National War Memorial Park in Islandbridge, organised by the British Legion.

In November, Patrick Pearse's 75th birthday anniversary was celebrated in the Mansion House in Dublin.

Mrs Aine Ceannt (nee Brennan), widow of Eamon Ceannt, (Commandment 4th Battalion, signatory of the 1916 Proclamation), died at St Josephs (her Churchtown home) in February. Mass was celebrated in Dundrum, and then burial in Deansgrange Cemetery (her husband is in the Republication plot in Arbour Hill, following his execution by the British Army in Kilmainham Jail in 1916).

Every year up to 1945 on St Patricks Day on 17th March, there was a military parade down O'Connell Street in Dublin, to commemorate the 1916 Easter Rising, but after the Second World War it became a commercial parade. Instead, there was a military parade on Easter Sunday from 1945 to 1966, the year the IRA and then Dublin Corporation demolished (by bombs) Nelsons Pillar in O'Connell Street.

During the Second World War, known as "The Emergency" in neutral Ireland, the Irish Army was augmented by volunteers organised into Local Defence Forces (LDF), dressed in military uniforms. After the war, the LDF'S were disbanded, but some members joined the official reserve army, the FCA. The memories of good times in the LDF's were to the forefront for many years afterwards, and some groups organised annual masses. For example, the Irish Independent of 28th June had a photo of a parade of former members of the 45th Rifle Battalion, from the Customs House to the Church of the Immaculate Heart of Mary, City Quay, led by the 26th (Fianna) Battalion, FCA.

The "Old IRA" cross in Harold's Cross dates from 1954.

The O'Donovan Rossa monument in St Stephens Green dates from 1954.

Catholic Religion

Up to at least the 1970's, the Catholic Church, or more precisely, its unelected clergy, dominated and controlled Irish society, and practically ran the country. Politicians gladly bowed to the Bishops wishes, and always adopted Church policy. Everyone, even priests, kissed the ring on the Bishops hand, while also genuflecting (half-kneeling). In matters of morality, homosexuality was illegal, as were contraceptives and abortion, even for non-Catholics.

John Charles McQuaid, who was the dreaded Primate of Ireland (including Northern Ireland) and Archbishop of Dublin, from 1940 to 1972, practically ruled the country with an iron fist, despite his humble origins in Market Street, Cootehill, County Cavan, adjacent to All Saints Protestant (Church of Ireland) church. His narrow rural upbringing shaped his ultra-conservative Catholic character and his hatred for all things Protestant. McQuaid had his palace in Drumcondra beside Holy Cross College (seminary), but also resided in his large secluded mansion in Killiney (Notre Dame de Bois, on the Military Road), using Notre Dame de Missions nuns as his domestic servants.

The 1950's was probably the period when the Church was at its most powerful, when every parish in the country had a fine big church, and a well-oiled machine collected contributions from rich and especially the poor.

Most schools were owned and run by priests, brothers and nuns, although the State paid the large salary bills, and part funded construction of the buildings.

The multitudes of priests went around the streets in long black ankle-length habits, wearing a white collar around the neck (called a dog-collar). Christian Brothers were almost identical to priests, except that their dog-collar was narrower. Most nuns had long (ankle-length) habits, and also a black shoulder-length cotton veil, and white front hair-band and bib, leaving only the face visible.

Practically every public and social event in Ireland was attended by the clergy in droves, often dressed in their fine Mass regalia, and nearly every meeting or committee was chaired by a Catholic clergyman.

Ireland specialised in producing huge numbers of priests and nuns, at enormous public expense, firstly to ensure that Ireland remained a Catholic country, and did not succumb to foreign influences, especially British ideas, and Communist leanings from other countries such as the Soviet Union/Russia, and secondly for export to the missions, where they could meddle in other countries affairs. The plain people of Ireland funded this enormous enterprise, by the "drip-feed method", with weekly church collections, Easter and Christmas Dues, etc. Hospitals and schools were built in far-off lands using "Pennies for the Black Babies" collections in Ireland, while Ireland itself wallowed in poverty and emigration for the masses. It was only when Ireland joined the European Economic Community (EEC) in the early 1970's, that large EEC grants were provided to upgrade Ireland's feeble and antiquated infrastructure, especially roads.

The newspapers never tired of including photos of priests and nuns. For example, the Irish Independent in June contained photos of 57 new priests after their ordination in St Patricks College, Maynooth, and 23 other ordinations in All Hallows College, Drumcondra, Dublin. Earlier in the month other priests were ordained in St Patricks in Carlow (34), St Kierans in Kilkenny (30), Oblates in Piltown, Kilkenny (2), St Patricks in Thurles (17), Pallottine in Thurles (2), St Peters in Wexford (16), and St Macartens in Monaghan (2).

Every week, the newspapers had a photo or at least an article, concerning priests and nuns sailing from Ireland to the Foreign Missions in Africa and China. Three leading groups were St Patricks Missionary Society, Kiltegan, County Wicklow, Society of African Missions (SMA), Blackrock, Cork, and Medical Missionaries of Mary, Drogheda, County Louth, to name but a few. There was a photo of SMA priests setting off to Nigeria, after the superior kissed the young priests feet, to wish them "God Speed". Another photo was of Maynooth Mission to China priests setting out from Cobh for the sea voyage to the Philippines.

Dublin was a city full of comforting religious smells and sounds – smells of candle-grease and incense wafting from the many churches, arising from numerous Masses and Benedictions every day, and bells ringing the Mass times and 12noon and 6.00pm Angelus. Many people took pride in attending daily Mass on their way to work, and most people Blessed themselves (made the "Sign of the Cross") when passing by any church – there was a superstitious belief of coming to some harm if you failed in this duty. Most people owned a set of Rosary beads, and also a missal, the latter a small book containing prayers and summaries of the church sacraments.

The church was the epicentre of peoples lives, not just for Mass on Sundays, but Mass on weekdays as often as possible. When inside, men removed their hats (in those days hats were an essential part of your wardrobe), and women kept their hats on, or else put on a silk headscarf. People called in all day long to recite the Rosary, and especially to "do the Stations of the Cross". The fourteen Stations were religious pictures or symbols on the inside of the church, depicting the last days of Jesus, from "Jesus is condemned to death" to "Jesus is laid in the tomb", and holy people said a prayer in front of each picture.

Weekends were busy for Confession, with all churches having at least a half-dozen Confession Boxes. These were three-compartment timber-built cubicles, with the priest sitting comfortably in the centre one, and he heard the confession (list of sins) of kneeling penitents, on alternate sides. Once granted Absolution, the penitent knelt elsewhere in the church and "did his or her penance" comprising recitation of a decade of the Rosary (or more decades for the really bold parishioners!). By this means, the priests got to know everything that was going on in the parish.

In Harold's Cross, Sunday Masses were at 7.45, 8.30, 9.15, 10.00, 10.45, 11.30, and 12.15. Attendance at one of these Masses was compulsory, and failure to attend would be noticed by nosy neighbours and reported, resulting in a visit from the priest to your house. Weekday Masses were at 7.30, 8.00, 10.00am. Holidays of Obligation were similar to Sundays, when Catholics must attend Mass, and in both cases, must abstain from servile work (therefore, shops, offices, and other workplaces, were closed).

"Plenary Indulgences" were granted to Catholics on various Feast Days, only if you went to Confession and received Holy Communion at Mass.

The Church had a litany of special days, such as Ember Days (4 Wednesdays, 4 Fridays, 4 Saturdays), and Rogation Days (3 days before Feast of the Ascension).

Religion even extended to peoples diet, such as not eating meat on Fridays, and having fish instead (which was no bad idea in itself). Everyone had to fast (abstain from food) from midnight on Saturday if going to Holy Communion on Sunday, which was later changed to a fast of at least one hour before receiving Holy Communion.

"Flag Days" were not political events, but fund-raising activities for churches and associated charities. Sporting a small sticker indicated to the public that you were a generous person, even if you only slid a farthing into the cardboard collection box. The annual Society of St Vincent de Paul flag days were the Saturday and Sunday towards the end of October.

"Sales of Work" were used widely by religious orders to raise money, and were well supported. There was an annual Sale of Work in the Mansion House in aid of the Oblate Fathers Missionary Fund. The laity donated items for sale (tinned food, toys, books, plants, etc), and then paid a small fee into the Sale to buy others peoples unwanted items.

Surprisingly, Dublin never had a Cathedral (only a "temporary" St Marys Pro-Cathedral) which could easily have been officially re-named the Cathedral in the Archbishop McQuaid era.

Marian Year

1954 was designated by the Pope as Marian Year, to honour Mary (Our Lady), mother of Jesus Christ, and wife of Joseph. Baby girls born in 1954 were often named Mary, while Joseph was a popular boys name that year.

This was the first time in the history of the church that there was a Marian Year, although there was another one from June 1987 to

August 1988, which generally went unnoticed (except in Fermoy, County Cork).

The Marian Year was formally opened on the 8th December 1953, with High Mass in St Patricks Cathedral, Armagh, and High Mass in St Marys Pro-cathedral, Dublin. On the 8th December, 1954, the Pope officially closed the Marian Year from his sick bed, and special Masses were conducted all over Ireland.

During this special year, Catholics were expected to honour Our Lady, by reciting the Rosary, both in private and in public, as often as possible. Everyone possessed a set of Rosary Beads, which was like a necklace, with beads representing prayers, in order to keep track of the number of times you recited the prayer, especially the Hail Mary.

The Rosary consists of five decades. Each decade comprises, one Our Father, ten Hail Marys, and one Glory Be, as follows:

Our Father, who art in Heaven, hallowed be Thy name, Thy kingdom come, Thy will be done on earth as it is in Heaven, give us this day our daily bread, and forgive us our trespasses, as we forgive those who trespass against us, and lead us not into temptation, but deliver us from all evil, Amen.

Hail Mary, full of grace, the Lord is with thee, blessed art thou amongst women, and blessed is the fruit of thy womb, Jesus. (Recited by the priest or leader of the prayers in a group setting).
Holy Mary, Mother of God, pray for us sinners, now and at the end of our lives, Amen. (Recited by the other people).

Glory be to the Father, and to the Son, and to the Holy Ghost, as it was in the beginning, is now, and ever shall be, world without end, Amen.

Hundreds of Marian Shrines in public spaces, usually a statue of Our Lady, sprang up all over Ireland, and were generally officially dedicated and blessed by the local clergy, and sometimes by the bishop. Thereafter, the locals recited the Rosary at the shrine, initially every evening, and then maybe once a week. Such statues were often painted white and blue.

Harold's Cross parish church was built in 1938, and named "Our Lady of the Rosary". Not surprisingly, a grey limestone statue of Our Lady of the Rosary was erected in Mount Drummond Square by local residents in 1954, carved by local sculptor, P. Crowe of 10 Emmet Street. A white marble statue was unveiled at Priory Square by the priests of the Rosary Church, Fr Brady PP, Fr Allen, Fr Flood, Fr Purcell, and Fr Browne, accompanied by "Faith of Our Father" played by the Rosary Pipe Band.

At the Curragh Army Camp (Barracks) in Kildare, the foundation stone was laid in 1954 for a statue of Our Blessed Lady, Queen of the Most Holy Rosary. Designed by Prof. F. Herkner of the National College of Art in Kildare Street, Dublin, the 8 feet high bronze statue was cast in Germany, and unveiled in 1956. The inscription simply says "Sancta Maria".

The Marian Shrine, Our Lady Queen of Peace, outside Broadstone Railway Station, was paid for by CIE workers, and like their trains, arrived ahead of schedule, in May 1953 to be exact!

The Marian Shrine in Ballinspittle, County Cork (near Kinsale), was typical of the statues erected across Ireland in 1954. However, in 1985 it became world-famous as the "Moving Statue" after a few local boys claimed to have seen the statue sway. Crowds flocked to the grotto, but it failed to become a site of pilgrimage like Knock.

May was the month every year when Our Lady was adored. Every single parish in the country had its May Procession, when a statue of Our Lady was carried on a small platform by the priests around the streets, followed by hundreds of parishioners, often grouped into Sodalities and Confraternities with individual colourful banners. Bunting and flags hung from all the houses and lamp-posts. The statue of Our Lady was officially crowned, with a real crown and veil, and paraded again, to the accompaniment of hymns played through loudspeakers. Every house had its own internal little statue of Our Lady, and a bunch of flowers, especially from the lilac bush. Being the Marian Year meant that the crowning of Our Lady was a huge social event. One wonders how the minority Protestants felt about these ceremonies, but no doubt some joined in the festivities.

In the city centre on 16th May, Archbishop McQuaid officiated at Benediction at a temporary altar built on the steps of the Pro-

Cathedral, and then 25,000 people paraded amidst flags and bunting through O'Connell Street, singing "The Lourdes Ave", and reciting the Rosary, while loudspeakers on lamp posts broadcast the proceedings from the Pro-Cathedral. Army trumpets sounded a Royal salute, whilst the crowds on O'Connell Street knelt.

From May 8th to 15th, various factories participated in an Industrial Tribute to Our Lady, the details of which were announced in April in the Catholic Commercial Club on O'Connell Street. Workers were encouraged to donate an hours pay for charitable use. Masses were held inside factories, e.g. Sunbeam Wolsey in Millfield, Cork (2,000 workers), General Textiles in Athlone (700 workers), Providence Woollen Mills in Foxford (Mayo), oratory of Irish Glass Bottle Company in Ringsend, Greenmount & Boyne Linen Company in Harold's Cross, Mc Donnells Margarine in Drogheda, P.J. Carroll & Company in Dundalk. The Tribute to Our Lady in Tonge & Taggart Foundry, Windmill Lane, comprised a Mass at a temporary altar, presided over by Archbishop McQuaid, accompanied by the choir of the Irish Glass Bottle Company.

On the 7th October, 1,000 army troops paraded to their Military Church at Arbour Hill, to commemorate Our Lady Queen of the Most Holy Rosary, patron saint of the Defence Forces, presided over by Archbishop McQuaid.

Knock Shrine to Our Lady

Even before the Marian Year of 1954, devotees of Our Lady visited her shrine in Knock, Co Mayo, often by way of a parish pilgrimage. Knock was a tiny village in 1879 when a few local people saw images on the gable wall of the old church (1828), on the evening of the 21st August, comprising Mary, Joseph and St John. A Commission of Enquiry that same year, and another in 1936, found the witnesses reliable, and the church promoted the site as a national place of pilgrimage, dedicated to Our Lady. Shops selling religious goods (statues, pictures, rosary beads, etc) soon sprang up along the main street, in addition to cafes, guest houses, etc. The large Basilica opened in 1976, and the present

Apparition Chapel abutting the gable wall of the old church was built in 1992, as a replacement for an earlier one used from 1940 to 1979.

Examples of pilgrimages during 1954 were 20,000 children visiting on the 9th May, including 8,000 carried by thirteen special trains into Claremorris (near Knock). On the Feast of the Assumption (15th August), 25,000 pilgrims visited, and hundreds remained all night outside the old church. 50,000 members of the Pioneer Total Abstinence Association (non-drinkers) made their pilgrimage on the 8th September. 2,000 army men made a Marian Year Pilgrimage to Knock on Rosary Sunday, 3rd October. The Dominican Pilgrimage to Knock took place on Sunday 10th October, with special trains and buses bringing thousands (total attendance was estimated at 10,000). On the 24th October, the CIE "Sodality of Our Lady" made their pilgrimage to Knock.

The Irish Independent newspaper published a photo of a Motor-Cycle Pilgrimage to Knock, leaving Merchants Quay in Dublin on March 17th, after the 25 men and machines were blessed by the Parish Priest.

In December, pupils of Loreto Convent in Balbriggan presented a tableau dedicated to "A century of Our Lady", describing apparitions at Knock and Fatima, accompanied by their choir, orchestra, and elocutionists.

In 2021, after much lobbying by the Irish Bishops, Pope Francis elevated the national shrine to International status, similar to Lourdes.

Lourdes & Fatima

Devotion to Our Lady was the reason many people made the pilgrimage to Lourdes in the south of France (founded in 1858), and Fatima in the centre of Portugal (founded in 1916), and the Marian Year was a golden opportunity to travel with groups.

Aer Lingus advertised the last flight to Lourdes for the Marian Year, leaving Dublin on 21st October, returning on 27th October, for a total of £41, including 6 days in Hotel de la Grotto. The package could be booked with American Express Co Inc, 116 Grafton Street, Dublin.

However, most pilgrims opted for the cheaper but much longer and harder route to Lourdes, catching the boat-train at Westland Row in Dublin, sailing from Dun Laoire to Holyhead, train down to London and on to Dover, ship to France, and train to Lourdes. Some overnight ships went direct from Dun Laoire to France, at additional cost.

Public Events

17th June was the Feast of Corpus Christi in the Catholic Church, and huge processions were organised in every parish. There was even one such procession in the Curragh Army Camp, County Kildare, with 2,000 troops. The processions involved the parishioners marching in formation through the streets of their neighbourhood, organised into the various sodalities and confraternities, including the Legion of Mary, Children of Mary, etc. Banners, flags and bunting adorned the houses and lamp-posts. Leading the procession was a battalion of priests, nuns, brothers, and altar boys, with the gold monstrance held aloft at the front. Often, there was an army group, or at least the FCA (reserve army), and of course the Garda Siochana band. Everyone dressed in their Sunday best suit of clothes, some wearing special colourful sashes. Children dressed in their First Holy Communion finery. Mass was usually celebrated in the Church first, and then the monstrance with the Blessed Host was carried outside, and at the end of the procession, Benediction, with smoking thuribles of incense, was held either in the church, or at a temporary altar elsewhere in the parish, the whole event lasting a few hours. Whether you liked it or not, everyone was swept away by the tide of public excitement and pageantry.

In December 1953, there was a big event in the Pro-cathedral to mark 300 years since the death of Archbishop Rinuccini, the first Papal Nuncio (ambassador from the Vatican in Rome) to Ireland. From 1930 to 1978, the nunciature was based in the former residence in the Phoenix Park of the British Under-Secretary of Ireland, provided by the Irish Government, and staffed by nuns (such as the Medical Missionaries of Mary), and nowadays used as the Ashtown Visitors Centre. The premises incorporated a late-medieval tower-house, only discovered in the 1980's when the surrounding Georgian wings were demolished by the Office of Public Works (OPW).

On the 27th July, 1954, the outgoing Papal Nuncio, Fr Gerald O'Hara, was given the Freedom of the City of Dublin in the Mansion House, in recognition of his good works since 1951. He had also received the Freedom of Limerick on the 25th June.

On 8th August, the new Papal Nuncio, Fr Albert Levame, was welcomed at Dublin Airport by Archbishop McQuaid, Liam Cosgrave (Minister for External Affairs), and Alfie Byrne (Lord Mayor of Dublin, who was known far and wide for his hearty handshake). On 31st August, there was a big reception in the Pro-cathedral to welcome him, with flags and bunting adorning the streets. In October, he was welcomed again by Archbishop McQuaid at a Liturgical Reception in St Patricks Seminary in Maynooth.

The newspapers added to the glamour and prestige of the Catholic clergy, recording every official event, even of a minor nature, with photos of the crowds, and the Bishop or Parish Priest dressed up in their finery. Confirmation and First Holy Communion groups often made the front page. One October headline ran: "Bishop Back from Rome", reporting that the Bishop of Galway had just flown back from a three-week visit to Rome, Lourdes and Fatima, in reality back from his holidays. The following are examples of headlines and photos in the main newspapers:

Youth Clubs attend High Mass at Franciscan Friary, Church of Adam & Eve, Merchants Quay.

Photo of Garda parade to Annual Retreat in St Francis Xavier Church, Gardiner Street.

Photo in the Irish Press of 700 guests at the Catholic Truth Society (CTS) annual reception in the Gresham Hotel, attended by bishops, the Taoiseach, and the President.

Irish Press photo of 800 Old IRA veterans in Marian Year Parade to St Saviours Church, Dominick Street (Dominicans).

Photo of Cardinal Spellman, Archbishop of New York, saying Mass in Shannon Airport (in a converted office), on his way to Rome, for the funeral of Cardinal Duca.

Photo of Fr Bertrand Firzgerald OP, back home on holidays from Trinidad.

Photo of Knights of Malta at Conventual Mass in June, in St Marys, Haddington Road, in splendid costumes and carrying their banners.

Fr Agnellus Andrew, OFM, speaking in St Patricks Seminary, Maynooth, warned about the good and bad aspects of the new medium of television, which would soon be in Ireland.

On 7th April, Mass in University Church, St Stephens Green, for Catholic nurses, all in their nurses uniform.

On the 11th April, there was a photo in the Irish Independent, showing the Blessing of Palms in the Pro-Cathedral in Dublin by Archbishop McQuaid, while students from Clonliffe/Holy Cross College processed around outside, dressed in surplice and soutane, and the Palestrina Choir provided the music and hymns.

On the 4th July, the International Congress of Catholics was held in the Irish Hospitals Trust (Sweepstakes) in Ballsbridge, with 1,000 guests, and then 700 of these attended a reception in St Patricks Seminary, Maynooth.

25th July was the annual pilgrimage to Croagh Patrick in Mayo, attended by 50,000 to 60,000, with Masses in the oratory at the top.

On the 8th September, the new headquarters of the Workers Union of Ireland opened in the former Vaughans Hotel, 29 Parnell Square West, and dedicated to the Immaculate Heart of Mary, attended by St James Brass & Reed Band, and Dublin Fire Brigade.

24th October was Mission Sunday, and newspaper advertisements beseeched: "Join the Society for the Propagation of the Faith, 1 Cavendish Row. Annual fee 2/2d. Daily prayer: recite one Our Father, one Hail Mary, and say – St Francis Xavier Pray for us".

On the 28th November, the Pioneer Total Abstinence Association held a rally in the famous Theatre Royal in Hawkins Street.

Public Lectures

In January, the Ard Fheis of An Rioghacht (League of Kingship of Christ) dealing with Catholic Action, was held at 4 Merrion Square, Dublin.

The Aberdeen Hall in the Gresham Hotel in O'Connell Street was the venue for a talk (lecture) entitled "The Apparitions at

Beawraing", about the appearance of the Blessed Virgin Mary in Belgium. Fr Deery, the Parish Priest of Mount Merrion in County Dublin, was the speaker, and the proceeds were in aid of the Mount Merrion Building Fund (their new Church on The Rise). This was a social occasion, and only the well-healed and well-dressed would have paid to enter the glamorous Gresham Hotel.

The Queens Theatre in Pearse Street was the venue for a lecture by a visiting Belgian priest about religious persecution in Communist China, entitled "Mary in Red China".

In March, the Spanish Ambassador gave a lecture in the Gresham Hotel about Catholic Spain and its Shrines of Our Blessed Lady, organised by Rochestown College (Cork) Past Pupils Union (PPU).

Miscellaneous

The Dublin branch of the Catholic Young Mens Society (CYMS) held their Centenary Solemn High Mass in St Columba's Church, Iona Road, Glasnevin. Over 1,000 members, from 21 Dublin branches, marched with bands and banners from the Customs House in the city centre to Glasnevin, and the Mass was presided over by Archbishop McQuaid. In 1954 there were 1,700 members in Dublin, and 11,000 members in rural Ireland.

In 1954, an old house, Nullamore, in Milltown, was converted by Opus Dei (a conservative lay Catholic lobby group) into a hostel for 40 Catholic students attending University College Dublin (UCD) in Earlsfort Terrace (nowadays the National Concert Hall).

8th December 1954 was the centenary of the Proclamation of Dogma on Immaculate Conception by Pope Pius IX. This dogma was not official church teaching before 1854, and proclaimed that Mary herself was conceived and born without Original Sin, despite the fate of Adam and Eve in the Garden of Eden. Many people mistakenly think that the dogma refers to Mary conceiving Jesus by the action of the Holy Spirit (and not by sexual intercourse with Joseph).

"A Flood of Filth", was an editorial heading in the Irish Independent newspaper on 4th October, concerning childrens comics coming in to Ireland from America.

The Censorship of Publications Board was at 5 Lower Ely Place, next door to the magnificent Ely House, and still the headquarters of the "Knights of Saint Columbanus" (a secretive lay conservative Catholic lobby group). Fr Joseph Deery of Kilmacud & Mount Merrion Parish, was chairman of the Board in 1954, and 1,000 books were banned that year, including many written by famous Irish and overseas authors. There was also a Film Censors office at 12-16 Harcourt Terrace.

There was a June photo in the Irish Independent newspaper of crowds at Westland Row train station, on their way to the Dun Laoire ship to France, on the Marist Pilgrimage for the canonisation of Blessed Peter Chanel by Pope Pius XII on the 12th June, a French Marist priest who died in 1841 on the Pacific Island of Futuna. A small contingent flew from Collinstown Airport (nowadays called Dublin Airport), to Paris, where they joined the main contingent and headed to Rome overland.

New Churches & Schools

As usual, the Catholic Church was busy with building projects in 1954, and the newspapers were invited to take photos at the laying of the Foundation Stone, which was actually a low-level stone plaque with the name of the Bishop, Parish Priest, Architect and Builder. Examples include, St Canice Church in Finglas, Church of Assumption in Walkinstown, and St Josephs Church, East Wall.

The new Church of the Most Precious Blood was opened by Archbishop McQuaid in December 1953, in West Cabra (Fassaugh Avenue), and holds 2,000.

The new Church of Our Lady, Queen of Peace, in Merrion, opened on the first Sunday of the Marian Year on 13th December 1953. The 1½ ton bell, cast by Matthew O'Byrne, James Street, was blessed and hoisted up the round tower on 30th October 1954.

Our Ladys Oratory opened in February on the premises of Irish Glass Bottle Company in Charlotte Quay, Ringsend, and was built entirely by the workers.

There was a June photo in the Irish Independent of the Mount Merrion Confirmation class in front of the old Fitzwilliam mansion, which had been converted into a church and school (new church opened in 1956).

A new £10,000 Primary School was blessed by Archbishop McQuaid at the Sisters of St Joseph of Cluny at Mount Sackville, Chapelizod.

The new Synge Street primary school, Sancta Maria, was opened by Archbishop McQuaid, attended by the schools own 44th Battalion of the FCA.

In 1954, the design for a new church in Bird Avenue, Clonskeagh was approved, but was not the winner of the formal competition.

Our Lady of Lourdes Church, Sean McDermott Street Lower, opened in 1954, replacing the original "tin church" on the same site, which had been erected in the early 20th century.

The new St Audoens National School in Cook Street was opened by Archbishop McQuaid in December.

The new Nurses Home (six-storey, brick-faced) opened in the Mater Hospital, and was blessed by Archbishop McQuaid.

1950's Corpus Christi procession in Harold's Cross. (Courtesy of Oliver Maher).

Marian Year marble statue of "Our Lady" in Corrib Road, Kimmage, with Mount Argus just visible on left side..

Marian Year limestone statue of "Our Lady" in Mount Drummond Square, Harold's Cross. Cathal Brugha Barracks in background..

Domestic Life

Accommodation

Dublin was small and compact in 1954. The population of the city and suburbs was about 580,000, and 650,000 including county areas. Leinster had a population of 1.34 million, while the population of the entire country was 2.93 million. Dublin Corporation controlled the city area, and Dublin County Council looked after the outlying areas.

Contraception was un-heard of, and most families had at least six children, although quite a few had up to ten or even twelve children.

Thousands of small but good quality houses, with front and back gardens, had been built by Dublin Corporation in Crumlin in the 1930's and 1940's, and then Ballyfermot in the 1950's, all available to working-class tenants at cheap rents.

Dublin Corporation was also building blocks of flats in the city centre for its tenants, such as Hardwicke Street (beside St Georges Church) at an average cost of building of £2,000 each, which was very expensive.

Dublin Corporation completed 660 new 3-bed houses in St Annes Estate, Clontarf (it was formerly part of the Guinness estate), with 590 available to Corporation tenants, under a Rent-Purchase scheme. The purchase price was £1,625, but deducting the Government Grant of £275, and the Corporation grant of £275, left a balance of £1,075, and no need for a deposit. Corporation tenants could pay £2 1s 7d a week (including insurance & rates) for 35 years, and then own the house. Normally, Corporation tenants would pay up to £1 10s a week in rent for smaller dwellings, but never own the property. Unfortunately, there was not much interest from Corporation tenants, and the private sector bought the lovely houses.

The Dublin Artisan Dwellings Company (DAD) had been building small cottages (both single-storey and two-storey) in and around the city since the 1870's, and the company had its impressive

26

offices at 12-13 South William Street. These dwellings were rented to skilled workers, and were in high demand despite the absence of gardens.

Most other people rented a flat (nowadays called a luxurious apartment), from a small private landlord, and very few people owned their own home. For example, Harry Lisney & Son were advertising flats to let in September from £3 a week, and houses from £3/10 a week.

Irish Estates Ltd, a subsidiary of Irish Life Assurance Co Ltd, was in the process of building and letting flats in Mespil Estate near Leeson Street Bridge, all of which were furnished by William J. Hicks, and leased to good tenants.

Many country girls from rural Ireland, who worked in the bloated Civil Service, stayed in religious-run hostels during the week, such as the Mercy Hostel (Young Womens Christian Association or YWCA) in 64 Lower Baggot Street, Sancta Maria Hostel in 75/76 Harcourt Street, De La Salle University Hall at 2-4 Ely Place Lower, University Hall (Jesuits) at 28a Hatch St Lower, Catholic Girls Hostel & Servants Registry at 19 Parnell Square North, Loreto Hall at 77 St Stephens Green (female students of UCD), St Kevins House at 42 Parnell Square West (residence for Catholic girls, and included the Kevin Barry Memorial Hall).

However, most country people opted to rent small bed-sitting-rooms and flats in the big old houses of Rathmines and Drumcondra, Mountjoy Square, Merrion Square, St Stephens Green, and surrounding streets, and also above shops in the city centre.

The privately-developed Greenhills Estate on Cromwellsfort Road was being built in 1954, with the houses costing £2,045, less the Government Grant of £275, leaving a total outlay of £1,770. The Deposit was £100, and County Council loans/mortgages were available for the balance of £1,670. Central heating consisted of a tubular back-boiler in the fireplace.

Other private housing estates being built in 1954 were Laurel Park Estate in Clondalkin (£2,000, less grant of £200), Turret Road in Palmerstown (£1,700 net), Ashton Park in Monkstown (£2,125 - £2,300), Sunnyside Estate on Vernon Avenue in Clontarf (4-bed semis for £2,450 by Collen Bros), Wynberg Estate on Stradbrook Road in

Blackrock (4-bed houses for £2,175, built by J.J. Jennings), Nutley Lane in Donnybrook (Borough Builders - £3,500), Landscape Estate in Churchtown.

The Army was building 88 new houses for married soldiers on Blackhorse Avenue, opposite McKee Barracks. For this development, the builder used newly-imported Blackwood Hodge mechanical swing-shovels (later replaced by the JCB excavator).

Dublin in the 1950's was full of orphanages, Industrial Schools, Reformatories, Magdalene laundries, and similar institutions, both Catholic and Protestant, providing very basic accommodation for the most unfortunate and vulnerable members of society.

Tramps and beggars could be accommodated in the Salvation Army Mens Hostel at 31a York Street (off the west side of St Stephens Green), or in "Back Lane", off Nicholas Street near Christchurch Cathedral, the latter hostel run by St Vincent de Paul, or the Iveagh Hostel in Bride Road (off Patrick Street) sponsored by the Guinness family.

Kitchen Appliances

Most people didn't have a fridge, but Frigidaire (4 cubic feet for £59) was aimed at more affluent people. The ESB had a fridge for £30 cash, or a hire purchase agreement (HP). Instead, most people used a "safe", a cupboard on stilts, with a wire mesh front door to allow air circulation. However, people generally shopped daily in their local shops, so a fridge was not really essential.

Gas cookers were the norm, but the unlit gas was poisonous and deadly if it escaped. They were well built to last a lifetime (never requiring repair or maintenance), of enamelled cast-iron, with oven, four rings, toasting area under hob, dish rack at very top, and a special spark-operated hose at the side for lighting the jets. There was no contract for the gas supply, since every house had a coin-operated gas meter (which took a shilling), which was emptied periodically by the Gas Company.

The ESB sold electric cookers from £25.2.6, while GEC electric cookers were £37.

Rayburn cast-iron ovens (which also supplied hot water) were manufactured by Waterford Foundry, cost upwards of £56.15s, and were available from Brooks Thomas, 4 Sackville Place, off O'Connell Street. Hammond Lane Iron Foundry, 111 Pearse Street, also made cast-iron cookers/ranges, and likewise Aga.

Most families did not have washing machines, and clothes were hand-washed, usually in the big white Belfast sink, using washing powders such as Rinso, Tide, Surf, Lux, or Persil. Clothes were hung out in the garden to dry, or indoors on timber "clothes horses". The wealthy might buy a Servis washing machine for £37.16.

"Vim" powder was used for cleaning cookers, saucepans, sinks, etc. A tub of "elbow-grease" would also have been welcome, but has yet to be invented!

The kitchen press (cupboard) usually contained a bottle of Dettol disinfectant, Nugget boot/shoe polish, and Mansion floor polish (to protect the floor linoleum). A roll of Flypaper was common, comprising a strip of sticky tape hung from lampshades to catch flies.

Food

Most housewives had a colourful "apron" to protect their clothes from food splashes and loose flour, since baking bread, cakes and buns was a regular activity.

The kitchen of 1954 would contain a "breadbin", a large circular metal container, to hold pans of white bread (no sliced bread yet for most people).

Butter was expensive, and therefore most people used Stork margarine on their cut slice of bread (made by W & C McDonnell in Drogheda and Dublin), costing 1/7 a lb.

Most of the food brands which are considered "modern" in 2021 have been around for many decades, as the following examples show.

Breakfast usually comprised a bowl of hot porridge (called "stirabout" in rural Ireland). Gradually cold cereals crept into the home, especially Kelloggs Corn Flakes, made under licence by Brown & Polson, Mount Tallant Avenue, Harold's Cross, which cost 11½ d for the regular 6 oz size, or 1/9 for a large 12 oz size.

Little Chip marmalade could be spread on your bread at breakfast time, or Chivers jams at other meals (the latter made at the Beech Hill factory Clonskeagh).

Most people cooked fresh vegetables, but Green Isle were producing canned meat and vegetables, and Crosse & Blackwell also made tinned soups (part of Williams & Woods).

Donnellys made skinless sausages, with a packet of 12 costing 2/- (a florin).

Every table had a small pot of freshly-made Colmans mustard for use on ham/bacon, YR sauce (brown colour), and Saxa salt. Bisto gravy was popular on meat dishes. Chef Salad Cream was a must on lettuce, long before we heard of mayonnaise.

The making of a cup of tea was a ritual, long before tea-bags were invented. A teapot (tea kettle) of water was boiled on the gas cooker, and a small quantity of loose tea-leaves was added, and the mixture allowed to "draw" (steep or soak) for a few minutes, before a cup of tea could be poured directly into your cup. Sometimes a little metal strainer was placed over the cup to collect stray tea leaves. Some people had a slightly more genteel way, by pouring hot water into a stoneware teapot on the table, then adding the tea-leaves, and allowing the mixture to "draw", although a tea-cosy (woolly hat) would be required to prevent the pot cooling during the meal. Often, the main teapot of the house would be on the cooker all day, with extra tea-leaves added occasionally, so that there was always a lovely smell of tea in the house.

The Tea Council of Ireland had advertisements simply asking consumers to drink Tea – no brands mentioned. Among the brands available in 1954 were Musgraves (Cork based), and Lyons Green Label. Lyons Tea had ads featuring the Black & White Minstrels, white people painted black, with only white eyes and mouth showing (no longer PC - politically correct). Coffee was less popular than tea, but Nescafe was a favourite.

Other hot drinks were Frys Cocoa, and Horlicks (bedtime drink) – the latter made by Johnson Bros in Poddle Park, Kimmage.

Pint-sized glass bottles of milk were delivered very early in the morning, and left on your doorstep (and the previous day's empty bottles collected) by motor and electric vans, and sometimes by horse and cart. Every bottle of milk had a one-inch topping of cream. Orange or silver metal foil caps sealed the bottle, although occasionally birds could pierce these and drink the cream.

Tap water was the most popular cold drink, and of course, free. Other drinks included Ribena, Lucozade, and occasionally Halls Wine for good health.

Jacobs were the main supplier of biscuits, such as Fig Rolls, "Marie" (1/10 lb), Ginger Nuts, and of course, Cream Crackers (half pound packets were 1/0½, loose crackers were 1/10 per lb). Gateaux Cakes (made in Finglas) were popular.

Tayto crisps (cheese & onion flavour) was started by Dubliner Joe "Spud" Murphy in O'Rahilly Parade, off Moore Street in the city centre, in 1954. They moved to Mount Pleasant Industrial Estate in Rathmines in 1956, and opened a sister factory in Tivoli Avenue in Harold's Cross in 1961.

Baby food included Farley rusks (a soft thick biscuit), Johnson Baby Powder, and Cow & Gate Milk Food.

Sittingroom

The sittingroom was plainly furnished, with armchairs around the coal fire, although some people had a two-bar electric fire (£3 15s). Esso Blue paraffin heaters might also be used.

A square of carpet might be provided instead of linoleum, with the floorboards around the carpet stained a dark colour. Most families had a sweeping brush for cleaning the floors, but a few people could afford a Hoover Vacuum Cleaner (£16.16.0). Philips also made vacuum cleaners, and in April, both Hoover and Philips were giving a 2-day free loan of a machine to prospective domestic customers.

Windows would be covered with see-through lace curtains, and also heavy night-time curtains, with a timber pelmet across the top of the window hiding the metal curtain track.

The sittingroom would be the place where the mother brought out her knitting-needles to darn holes in socks, and patch worn elbows in jumpers and cardigans.

Every home had a "wireless" (radio), which was regarded as the heart of the home, second only to a roaring coal fire in the livingroom. The radio was in fact plugged into an electrical socket outlet, but the radio waves floated into the house on fresh air, being received by special valves/tubes inside the radio, hence "wireless" reception. Most radios had long-wave and medium-wave, with an abundant selection of stations. Radio Eireann was on medium-wave, and the popular BBC Light was on long-wave. The Garda Siochana "squad cars" operated on short-wave, and occasionally their messages could be picked-up by the public: "Control to Alfa 4, or Romeo, etc. The radios were manufactured in Ireland by companies such as Murphy of Islandbridge, Pye of Dundrum, Philips of Clonskeagh, Bush or GEC, and sold by distributors such as Walkers of Upper Liffey Street. The latter company also sold Bush portable radios, with dry batteries, for 17 guineas. In January, 1954, the Fair Trade Commission held an enquiry into the sale and distribution of radios, noting that about 55,000 sets were sold per annum at 18 guineas a set.

In the first half of the 20th century, the gramophone (phonograph), playing "78" records (seventy eight revolutions per minute), was only to be seen in the homes of the very wealthy. In the middle of that century, it was still only the affluent who could afford a Record Player, playing Vinyl Records of classical music, or jazz, or popular artists such as Bing Crosby.

Pye Radio in Dundrum (now the site of the Dundrum Town Centre) mostly manufactured radios, but also produced a Hi-Fi record player called "The Black Box", retailing at 30 guineas (a lot of money). Mr Digby of Pye was reported in the newspapers as demonstrating the machine in the plush surroundings of the Shelbourne Hotel, playing 7 inch, 10 inch and 12 inch vinyl records. They also had a trade stand at the Spring Show in the RDS. Pye were also making Radiophones in 1954, being 2-way radios used by big companies with vans on the road (long before the modern mobile phone).

Long-playing records (LP's) had just been developed (only Singles available up to this time), and Philips Electrical Ireland were now manufacturing them, when a factory opened in Clonskeagh in September. This big Dutch firm was one of the first companies to be attracted into Ireland by the fledgling Industrial Development Authority (IDA). "His Masters Voice" (HMV) was the leading record producer.

Bedroom

O'Dearest mattresses were manufactured by O'Dea & Co, Wolfe Tone Street, Dublin. Bedclothes consisted of layers of wool blankets, finished off with a coloured "bedspread" or "eiderdown". Rubber hot-water bottles would be placed underneath the blankets just before getting into bed.

There was no built-in furniture, and most people possessed a wardrobe, dressing-table, and chest of drawers, generally of basic construction, but sometimes made with expensive hardwoods such as walnut, oak or mahogany.

The dressing table usually had some Max Factor lipstick, and Ponds Face Cream.

Bathroom

Showers had not yet been invented, so the bath was used once a week for a good scrub (nowadays called a "deep clean"), but it was also very relaxing and therapeutic. Children could be washed in the kitchen "Belfast sink", or in a big oval shaped steel tub positioned anywhere on the floor. Sunlight soap was popular, and likewise Lifebuoy, but some people used carbolic soap, which was cheaper but had a hospital smell. Hair-washing for adults was usually done in the kitchen sink or bathroom handbasin. There were no electric hairdryers, and in the Winter people knelt down and dried their hair in front of the coal fire. Girls with long hair had to spend the whole evening at this chore. Shampoo came in little plastic sachets, which could do a few heads, with brands such as Loxene, Silvikrin, Palmolive, and Vaseline.

Men used Gillette double-edged disposable blades for shaving, which came in packs of five, and these were inserted into a steel-handled razor. The shaving lather was obtained from a bar of soap, but some people could afford Palmolive shaving cream. Only the wealthy could afford a Remington Electric Razor, with cost £8.6.0. Hair oil for men, such as Brylcream, was an essential item.

SR Toothpaste and Colgate Dental Cream were popular. Kent toothbrushes ran a competition in 1954, the prize being a holiday in London for two, flying by Aer Lingus Viscount.

The medicine cabinet could be either in the kitchen or the bathroom, with supplies of Anadin, Aspro and Alka-Seltzer for headache. Senna pods (in hot water) were used for constipation, as were Beechams Pills or California Syrup of Figs. Andrews Liver Salts, and Maclean Stomach Powder and Tablets were used for indigestion, although Milk of Magnesia was more popular for children, especially after eating raw cooking apples. A dab of Iodine lotion was a must to heal cuts and scratches on childrens legs and arms, or some Vaseline cream, and fine combs were used to search for lice in their hair.

Dettol (made by Recketts of Edmondstown Road in Rathfarnham) and Jeyes fluid, were used to disinfect the home, while FLAK "DDT" powder dealt with flies, fleas, nits, lice, woodworm, bed bugs, cockroaches, and even maggots in sheep!

Hall

This was the location of the latest status symbol, the telephone, since very few people had a private phone. The new Sutton Telephone Exchange for the Department of Posts & Telegraphs (P & T) was a newsworthy event, boasting that already there were 720 subscribers in that locality.

Most people relied on coin-operated public telephone boxes, free-standing cubicles made of concrete, painted cream and green, with one positioned on most street corners. Long-distance calls (trunk-calls) had to be routed via telephone exchanges, manned by an army of female operators. The Department of Post & Telegraphs had a trunk-call exchange at 11-17 Exchequer Street.

Urgent messages were sent by "telegram" ("telegraph"). The sender went to a Post Office, filled in a form with the message, which was expensive (dependant on the number of words), and this was relayed to the GPO by overhead telegraph wires around the city, a slip of paper was filled in, and dispatched to the recipient either by bicycle around town, or a motorbike to the suburbs. The new invention of a "fax" machine was introduced in Dublin in 1954, and was used by the Department to send telegrams from local Post Offices to the GPO, within a range of 15 miles.

The hall was the location of the electrical fuseboard. "Blown" fuses could be either replaced, or mended with special pieces of fuse wire, (although in emergencies some people used a strip of silver cigarette foil!). "Solus" light bulbs were used throughout the house, which company was founded in 1935, and based in Corke Abbey, Bray.

Coats and hats were hung on the wall in the hall, and mens galoshes were kept nearby – these were rubber slippers which were fitted over existing leather shoes as a protection in wet weather.

The Baby's pram was kept in the hall, and with large families the norm, a strong Walker pram was a must, ranging in price from 10 guineas to 25 gns. Walkers even had a pram show in the Mansion House in February.

Most homes had a "Child of Prague" statue somewhere in the house, in addition to a "Sacred Heart" picture, with maybe a little red electric bulb underneath.

Back Garden

The clothes line was essential before the days of drying machines. And before the invention of disposable "pampers", mothers washed the baby's cotton nappies, and re-used them for years.

Many families had a "swing", which kept children occupied for many hours. Playing basic football was always a favourite with the boys in the family, and sometimes the "tom-boys".

A striped canvas folding deckchair was common, when parents tended to stay at home for most of their free time.

Of course, the grass had to be kept trim in season, and most people had a push mower, although the wealthy might opt for a Qualcast motor mower, with 16 inch cutting width, costing £43/10. Black & Decker power tools were also available for the DIY enthusiast.

Toys

Expensive Hornby train sets by Meccano, and Scalectric tracked racing cars, were much in demand from Santa, in addition to dolls houses, scooters and tricycles, roller skates, skipping ropes, Yo-Yos, and occasionally a Rocking Horse. Lego was extremely popular, in addition to board-games such as Snakes & Ladders. Children loved playing simple games of cards, which was a great way of improving their mental arithmetic. Jig-saws were at the heart of childrens free-time in Winter, in addition to a plentiful supply of "mala" (plasticene). Boys revelled in playing with "Dinky" metal cars, and bigger moving cars and trucks with a wind-up spring. Little plastic soldiers and farm animals were plentiful. Simple marbles were very popular with boys, either for indoor or outdoor games.

Most children adored "comics", whether new or a swap, with such titles as Beano, Dandy, Hotspur, Bunty, etc. Other children loved reading books, especially those by Enid Blyton, and the local library stocked endless supplies. Titles included Noddy, The Famous Five, Biggles, Billy Bunter, etc.

Shopping

Irish people in 1954 dressed far better than nowadays, and casual clothes were never worn in public, except by the many tramps roaming the cities and towns. Men and women, and even boys and girls, definitely had "style", and in fact, enhanced the streets and public transport. Most men wore hats in public, and used Brylcream hair oil to flatten unruly hair, and add a sheen. Even the street urchins in Dublin city centre wore flat caps. Women wore colourful head scarves in public, usually silk, with nice floral or abstract patterns.

Before the advent of Supermarkets and Office Blocks in the 1960's, and Apartment Blocks in the late-1980's, Dublin city centre was a thriving mix of every type of shop at street-level, and thousands of small businesses and offices occupied the upper floors of city centre buildings, in addition to a substantial number of flats (apartments). The big department stores, such as Brown Thomas and Arnotts, originally had dormitories for their shop-assistants on the upper floors. All shops closed for half a day every week, usually on Wednesdays, or maybe Saturday (Todd Burns in Mary Street was a Saturday). 8th December was the annual invasion of Dublin by rural shoppers, who arrived by special trains. In 1954, the 8th December was on a Wednesday, so the usual half-day changed to Tuesday.

Many shops had retractable canvas awnings, which shielded the window contents from the damaging glare of the Irish sun, and also protected pedestrians from inclement weather.

Caroline Mitchell had a column in the Irish Times in October, entitled "Around The Shops", reminding readers that McBirneys had a three-piece suite of two armchairs and a sofa for £39 10s (was £47 10s). Also 4 ft 6 inch spring interior mattresses for £8 12s 6d, and base for £4 15s. Mens wool gaberdine coats were £9 17s 6d.

At the end of November, Georges Street Christmas lights were turned on by Lord Mayor, Alfie Byrne. Pims Department Store in this street always had a great Christmas window display.

Germany presented a Christmas tree (and lights) to Dublin, and it was positioned in College Green.

Department Stores

Brown Thomas, 15,16,17 Grafton Street, was Dublin's most exclusive department store. The building became Marks & Spencer in 1994.

Switzers, 88-95 Grafton Street, was across the road from Brown Thomas, but was only a little cheaper. In April, 1954, the shop was advertising "Twilfit" girdles/corsets at 33/- to 42/- (made in Twilfit House, Jervis Street). The building became Brown Thomas in 1991.

McBirneys, 14-18 Aston Quay (between Aston Place and Prices Lane), was popular for drapery, furniture and household goods. The building is now called Hibernian House, and part occupied by Supervalu grocery supermarket.

Clerys, O'Connell Street, was owned by Denis Guiney, and was a household name throughout Ireland. In September 1954, they had Fur Coat Week – beaver, mink, musquash, Persian lamb, ermine, squirrel, etc – when fur coats were a status symbol amongst Irelands wealthy families.

Arnotts, 9-15 Henry Street, was the big draw of this street, and was on a par with Switzers.

Roches Stores, 54-62 Henry Street, with warehouse in 1-5 Denmark Street, was a favourite with Dubliners, because of its good value for standard domestic items. They had branches in Cork (Patrick Street), and Limerick (O'Connell Street). In recent decades, the company was taken over by Debenhams Department Stores.

Todd, Burns & Co, 47 Mary Street (drapery) and 17-21 Mary Street (furniture and carpets). In October 1954, they had an in-house demonstration of rug-making at home, with supplies of wool, canvas, needles. Since 1969 the building has been occupied by Penneys Department Store.

O'Dea, 41-48 Wolfe Tone Street, were house furnishers and makers of Odearest mattresses, and adjoined the former Mary Street Picture House. Now AXA insurance company offices.

Denis Guiney (who also owned Clerys) was the big attraction in Talbot Street, because of his lower prices, with outlets in 16 Talbot Street (clothes), 22-23 Talbot Street (furniture & carpets), and Guiney & Co, 79/80 Talbot Street (clothes).

Boyers drapery, 20/22 North Earl Street (furniture in 4 Cathedral Street), and Bolgers drapery, 23/24 North Earl Street, were both popular, being near to O'Connell Street. Hickey Fabrics, 6 North Earl Street, was the place to buy material to make your own dresses and curtains.

Georges Street was a major shopping street, with Pims (75-84) being the biggest store, in addition to Cassidys and Winstons. Winstons (ladies fashions) opened a small shop in the street in 1930, but in 1954 acquired the adjoining Red Lion Hotel and Pub at the corner of Stephens Street, and when converted that same year, called it Winstons Corner (41-46). A special feature was their Outsize Department on the ground floor, for ladies with larger figures. Winstons was later converted into Dockrells Hardware shop.

Camden Street was popular, with stores such as Gorevans (1-4 Lower Camden Street), Nicholls (43 Lower Camden Street), and also Douglas in nearby 17-19 Wexford Street.

Lees (Edward Lee & Co) was popular, with stores at 48 Mary Street, 282/284 Lower Rathmines Road, 22-24 Upper Georges Street in Dun Laoire, 2 Goldsmith Terrace in Bray.

Frawleys of 34/36 Thomas Street, for drapery, beds and curtains, was a mainstay of the Coombe, but closed in 2007.

Whilst the big department stores sold drapery, furniture, carpets, household goods, and more, Woolworths was in a league of its own. F. W. Woolworth & Co Ltd (Frank Winfield Woolworth) was a big American chain, founded in 1879, with 3 outlets in Dublin, 65-68 Grafton Street (the first, opened in 1914), 18-21 Henry Street, 89 Georges Street, Dun Laoghaire, and others around the country. Grafton Street and Henry Street had cafes, operating from 10.30am to 6.30pm. Thomas Street (126/127) opened in 1954, but closed in the 1960's. Grafton Street had a lovely old façade, which was replaced by a modern one in the 1960's. These stores sold ice-cream cones, pick 'n mix sweets, biscuits, scarves, handkerchiefs, household small items, soaps, crockery, postcards, makeup, and even some groceries from the 1950's. The group closed suddenly in 1984.

Men's Outfitters

Men wore shirts with detachable collars (for ease of washing), and Clubman shirts came with two collars. Ties were standard for most men, and even workmen on building sites wore ties under their cardigans or pullovers. Most men and older boys wore sports-jackets, or sometimes the top half of their only suit.

Shoes could last a decade, because shoemaker shops "soled and healed" worn parts. Galoshes (rubber slippers) were used in wet weather over shoes to protect them. Sandals were worn a lot in the Summer, preventing sweat and promoting healthy feet.

Most boys wore short pants up to the age of twelve, or even longer, with socks up their knees, and many boys also wore caps, often with their school emblem – even the Christian Brothers schools went in for uniforms and caps. The wearing of long pants signified the transition to being a youth (teenager).

Towards the end of the 1950's, duffel coats, in black or sometimes fawn, were becoming popular, featuring big and prominent timber pegs/buttons, because of reasonable prices and hard-wearing.

Many men sported the "fainne", a tiny gold ring pinned to their lapels, boasting that they spoke the Irish language. Schoolboys even wore them, but may not have been entirely up to scratch.

The Pioneer Pin was another must-have accessory for the trendy male, indicating that they were members of the Pioneer Total Abstinence Association, and had an aversion to alcohol. These pins were handed out in secondary schools, including to young lads who only had enough pocket-money for sweets.

The main mens clothing chains, with branches around the city centre, were Burtons, Best, Kingstons, and Hipps. Montague Burton will always be associated with his outstanding cream-tiled building at the corner of Dame Street and South Great Georges Street, built in 1920, nowadays sharply contrasting with the nearby appalling office block on South Great Georges Street which was built on the site of the famous Pims Department Store. The Blackrock Tailoring Company was at 18 Chatham Street, at the corner of Balfe Street, a big stand-alone store. Other shops included Kevin & Howlin, at 39 Nassau Street, and Kennedy & McSharry, at 4 D'Olier Street and 24 Westmoreland Street. O'Connors, 21 Upper Abbey Street, specialised in workmens overalls, and then jeans in later decades.

Women's Outfitters

Women in general dressed very well in 1954, adding colour and style to the entire city centre. Denim jeans were not yet in vogue, and cotton slacks were not acceptable in public. Lively hats and colourful handbags were the norm. Nylon stockings (such as Bear brand) converted white legs into tanned sun-drenched limbs. Stiletto heels were worn by most women, in order to show-off their lovely calf-muscles and slim ankles, although ruined lino floor coverings in the home, and parquet hardwood floors in public buildings. Women were fitter, since they walked a lot, and ate smaller wholesome meals. Women were very proud of their feminine curves, and were assisted in this direction by the use of the almost universal use of corsets (girdles). These were torture garments made with elasticated fabrics fitted with a series of vertical strips of steel springs or thin bones, designed to hold in expanding tummies. Gossard was a well-known brand at the time. Leethams Ltd had their factory in Twilfit House, Abbey St/Jervis St, making "Twilfit "corsets ("it will fit" meaning the new figure-hugging dress will fit if a corset is worn underneath), which sold for 33/- to 42/- in Switzers Department Store (and elsewhere).

Obviously, the big department stores had extensive ladies departments, but specialist shops offered the latest European fashions, and more personal attention. Famous Irish fashion designers in 1954, including Sybil Connolly, Irene Gilbert, Neilli Mulcahy (daughter of Richard Mulcahy), and Miriam Woodbyrne, helped propel the demand for unique dresses and women's outfits.

Most of the ladies fashion shops in 1954 were in South Great Georges Street, such as Cassidys (53-57), Kelletts (corner of Exchequer

Street), Gleesons (45), Colette Modes (66), Macey (69-72 - immediately south of Pims Department Store). Nearby was Nicholls of Exchequer Street, and Slyne, 71 Grafton Street (specialised in gowns for balls). North of the River Liffey could be found Menzies (49 Henry Street), Sloweys Outsize Shop (45/46 Henry Street), Madame Nora, 6/7 Upper O'Connell Street, Cassidys (9 Lower O'Connell Street), and The Silk Mills, (21-27 Lower Dorset Street).

Fur coats, wraps, and scarves were signs of affluence, and a few shops specialised in selling, repairing and cleaning these expensive garments, such as Vard & Vince (1 South Anne Street), Charles Wayre, (73 South Great Georges Street), Swears & Wells (70 Grafton Street), and Barnardo (108 Grafton Street). There was even a fur farm in Dundrum (where the "old" shopping centre was later built).

Bookshops

Veritas at 7 Lower Abbey Street catered for Catholic religious books and artifacts. Veritas House was built on the site of the Union Chapel (Presbyterian), which was destroyed in the 1916 Easter Rising. In 1954, the building also housed the Catholic Truth Society of Ireland, and An Rioghacht (The League of the Kingship of Christ).

The Association for Promoting Christian Knowledge (APCK) was in 37 Dawson Street, and the Hibernian Bible Society was in 41/42 Dawson Street, both aimed at Protestant customers.

Easons at 40/41 Lower O'Connell Street, were general booksellers, and also publishers of Catholic prayer books and missals. The business included a Circulating Library, whereby books could be rented cheaply, in competition with public libraries.

Gill, 50 Upper O'Connell Street, sold books, and also dealt in church brasswork etc. Later, they were called Gill & Macmillan, book publishers, and are now Gill Books.

Browne & Nolan were in 41/42 Nassau Street, beside Jammets Restaurant, which bookshop included the building behind in 4-8 Adam Court, off Grafton Street. The business later moved to 56 Dawson Street.

Hodges Figgis was in 104 Grafton Street in 1893, 20 Nassau Street in 1923, and 6 Dawson Street in 1954. Nowadays they are in 56 Dawson Street, which was formerly Browne & Nolan bookshop, and before that, Brown Thomas department store, and even earlier was Drummonds Seeds.

Greenes Bookshop was in 16 Clare Street, including a Post Office, and only closed in recent years.

Fred Hanna, 28/29 Nassau Street (part of Morrison Chambers), was a legend in Dublin, dealing in new, second-hand, and college books. Now a big branch of Easons Bookshop. The Dublin Bookshop, 32 Bachelors Walk, was also owned by Fred Hanna.

George Webb, 5/6 Crampton Quay. This shop, and some other bookshops in Dublin, had tables in front, under the awning, displaying second-hand books, and were much loved by browsers and window-shoppers.

Combridge, 18 Grafton Street, dealt in books and stationery, and later ended up in Suffolk Street as fine art dealers (paintings and picture-framers). Eblana Books were at 46 Grafton Street.

James Duffy, 38 Westmoreland Street, sold books and religious goods, a bit like Veritas.

Helys stationery, 26-28 Dame Street were also printers, with their Acme Works on Dame Court directly behind the Stags Head pub.

Small suburban bookshops included Banba, at 119 Lower Clanbrassil Street, and 101 Upper Dorset Street.

International books published during 1954 included: "Live and Let Die" by Ian Fleming (later made into a James Bond film), "Lord of the Flies" by William Golding, and "Lord of the Rings" by Tolkien. The world-famous "Guinness Book of Records" was first published in 1955, although there was a free edition in 1954.

"My Left Foot", the autobiography of Christy Brown, was published in 1954, and tells the remarkable story of this severely-disabled Dublin author, who used only his foot to write and paint.

In October, 1954, Ernest Hemingway was awarded the Nobel Prize in Literature, for "The Old Man and the Sea". The generous prize was £12,500 plus a gold medal, and the official ceremony was held in December in Stockholm (Sweden).

On the 15th October, a plaque was unveiled at 21 Westland Row, in memory of Oscar Wilde: "Poet, dramatist, wit, Oscar Wilde, do rugadh sa teach seo 16/10/1854" (Irish for "was born in this house").

Specialist Shops

Victor Waddington Galleries, 8 South Anne Street. The Patrick Hall Exhibition was held here in October, with paintings costing between 20 and 30 guineas each (a guinea was £1/1s).

Gings Theatrical Stores, 3 Dame Street (just east of City Hall), sold costumes and wigs for actors and actresses in the theatre, and was ideally located opposite the Olympia Theatre.

Chemists confined themselves to mixing and measuring drugs and other ingredients, specifically for each customer's needs, since there were very few factory-made pills and potions. Most also sold rolls of Kodak and Ilford film to photographers, and then the chemist developed and printed the photos in their own "dark room". Dublin Pharmacy, 23 Fownes Street, had an optical department, where spectacles could be bought for 17/6d. Other chemists included Prices Medical Hall, 26 Clare Street, Hayes Cunningham & Robinson (HCR) at 12 Grafton Street (now Boots Chemists) and branches, Hamilton Long, 107 Grafton Street and 5 O'Connell St Lower. Dixon Hempenstall, 111 Grafton Street, were opticians, and specialised in mathematical instruments.

Noblett Confectionary, 52 Grafton Street (Gael Linn corner), and Lemons, 49 O'Connell St Lower, were a magnet for sweet lovers.

Millar & Beatty, house furnishers, 13/14 Grafton Street, and Cavendish furniture, 28 Grafton Street, sold nothing else but furniture. Secondhand furniture could be bought on the Liffey quays, such as Tormey Bros, 26/27 Ormond Quay Lower, who held an auction every Tuesday at 1.00pm. Tintawn Carpets had their showrooms at 13/14 South King Street, where you could buy a 9ft by 9ft carpet for £7 (known as a "square"), before the advent of fully-fitted carpets (meaning wall-to-wall).

Walpoles, 8-10 Suffolk Street, were manufacturers and retailers of linen, especially tablecloths, but also women's clothes.

The China Showrooms, 32/33 Lower Abbey Street, and Arklow Pottery, 39 Westmoreland Street, provided nice delft for the diningroom table.

Callaghan of 13-16 Dame Street specialised in supplies for the gentry who adored hunting (guns), riding (saddles), and fishing tackle.

Watches and jewellery could be obtained from H. Samuels (15 South Great Georges Street), Weirs (96 Grafton Street), West (102-103 Grafton Street), Hopkins & Hopkins (1 Lower O'Connell Street), McDowell (3 Upper O'Connell Street), and Ganter Bros (63 South Great Georges Street).

Estate agents included James Adam (19 St Stephens Green), Lisney (23 St Stephens Green), and Battersby (39 Westmoreland Street).

Good boots and shoes were essential, because most people walked a lot, and many went hiking in the Dublin mountains. Good shops were Saxone (a Scottish firm with various branches), Fitzpatricks, and Tylers. Clarkes of Dundalk manufactured shoes, and these were widely sold in their own shops.

Waltons Music Academy, 2,3,4 North Frederick Street, and 90 Lower Camden Street, was an institution throughout Ireland, and sold musical instruments and sheet music. In October 1954, they were demonstrating the Lincoln Organ in the O'Connell Hall, 42 Upper O'Connell Street (rear section of the Catholic Commercial Club). The company had a very popular sponsored radio programme, with the catchphrase "if you feel like singing, do sing an Irish song." The Emerald Girls Pipers Band, and City of Dublin Girls Pipers Band, were in the same premises as Waltons.

Pigotts of 112 Grafton Street were famous for pianos, radios, records, and gramophones. Likewise, McCullough, 56 Dawson Street, were popular. The two companies later amalgamated as McCullough Pigott in South Andrew Street. Gills, 14/15 Nassau Street, was also a good shop for pianos.

In December 1954, Eamon Andrews (then working for the BBC) officially opened a new Record shop at the corner of Grafton Street and South Anne Street.

Everyone communicated by letter and postcard, and Dublin had a few postal collections each day – you could post a letter in the morning, and receive a reply that afternoon. Most people used a cheap nibbed pen and a little bottle of black or blue ink (plus blotting paper!). The well-off used "fountain pens" with a re-fillable rubber tube containing ink (such as the "Parker 51" or a Conway Stewart pen). There were also some fancy but expensive Biros, looking like a fountain pen, with clip to hold it in the breast pocket of your jacket. The Pen Corner at 12 College Green dealt only in fountain pens and accessories.

Most people did not have a Bank account (and hence, no cheque-book), and paid cash for utilities such as electricity, gas, and coal. These companies had showrooms and cashiers in one locality in the city centre, near the bus routes, for example, Electricity Supply Board (ESB) at 40-43 Fleet Street, and Dublin Gas in D'Olier Street. All the coal importers were in Westmoreland Street and D'Olier Street, and even Andy Clerkin, Lord Mayor of Dublin, had his coal business in nearby 204 Pearse Street.

Hector Grey was a legend in his own lifetime, with the motto, "stack em high, and sell them cheap", dealing in similar goods as Woolworths, from 1 and 26 Upper Liffey Street. In 1954, he was advertising German cuckoo clocks, 21/1 post free. On Sunday mornings Hector became a street-seller, standing on a box near the north side of the Halfpenny Bridge, engaging in banter with the large crown of bargain-hunters. Walkers was beside Hector Grey in 27-29 Upper Liffey Street, although more upmarket, selling prams, bicycles, electrical goods etc - their annual pram show was held in the Mansion House.

Elverys, 47 O'Connell Street Lower (Elephant House), specialised in waterproof and sports clothing. They had a branch at 65/66 Dawson Street (corner of 34 Nassau Street), a nice 4-storey brick building. Nowadays, they trade from nearby Suffolk Street.

Long before the advent of modern Garden Centres, Dublin gardeners obtained their fertiliser, plants, bulbs, seeds, and implements from Seed Merchants, such as Rowan (51/52 Capel Street and 1,2,3 Westmoreland Street), Drummond (57/58 Dawson Street), Mackey (23 Upper O'Connell Street -beside the Gresham Hotel), and McKenzie (212/213 Pearse Street).

Most "thinking men" smoked a pipe, and every other man seemed to smoke cigarettes, with the result that their hands and mouths were never idle – it was simply a fashion craze. Hence, there were shops specialising in pipes, whilst tobacconists stocked cigarettes. John Purcell Ltd, 22 Westmoreland Street (facing directly on to O'Connell Bridge) sold pipes, tobacco, and souvenirs. Lafayette photographers were in the same building to the south of Purcells shop. Fox, 119 Grafton Street, sold cigars. Kapp & Peterson were in both 55 and 117 Grafton Street plus O'Connell Street, manufacturing and selling the best in pipes. Coady, 39 Dame Street, were tobacconists, and also sold Sweepstakes Tickets, with a lucky horseshoe on their shopfront.

Even before the invention of Spanish-sun package holidays in the 1960's, prosperous citizens liked to travel, using such travel agents as Thomas Cook (118 Grafton Street), Hewitts (D'Olier Street), and Twohig (8 Burgh Quay). Butlins (4-5 Trinity Street) catered for more modest holidays, including Portmarnock Holiday Camp. The Irish Tourist Board (13 Merrion Square) promoted Irish holidays.

The pawnbroker (Money Office) was an integral part of the retail landscape, providing small loans to poor people, with numerous shops around the city, denoted by "three brass balls" hanging outside what appears to be a second-hand jewellers. Famous names were Brereton, (108 Capel Street), and Kilbride (53 Clanbrassil Street Lower).

One important business consisted of street photographers such as Arthur Fields, who roamed around O'Connell Street, especially the Bridge, taking photos of locals and visitors, without obligation, which you could collect later from a nearby office.

Hardware

Maguire & Gatchell occupied 7-15 Dawson Street, extending back to South Frederick Street, and stocked an extensive range of hardware and homeware, arranged over a number of floors.

Thomas Lenehan & Co of 124/125 Capel Street was more modest, and also sold the Tilley radiator and iron, which used paraffin oil, for those who had still not adjusted to electricity.

McQuillan, 36 Capel Street, was the best place for tradesmen's tools, and is still trading here.

Wigoders, 75 Talbot Street, sold wallpaper of every description, and also paint.

The name, Dublin Glass & Paint Company, 41 Middle Abbey Street, speaks for itself, and also engaged in stained-glass for churches.

Noyeks, 200 Parnell Street, was great for sheet timber, such as plywoods. Following a fire in 1972, eight people were killed.

The Irish Agricultural Wholesale Society, 151-156 Thomas Street (offices) and 35 James Street (shop), specialised in everything for the farmer.

Markets

Dublin Corporation's charming red-bricked "Fruit, Vegetable and Egg Market" and Fish Market, was bounded by Mary Street Little and Arran Street East. This was a wholesale market, and from dawn was thronged with shopkeepers from all over Dublin. Only recently closed.

The Iveagh Markets, 21-27 Francis Street, was an indoor version of Moore Street, with a variety of street traders (hawkers). Second-hand clothes were to the front, and fruit & vegetables to the rear. Has been closed for years.

The huge Dublin Cattle Mart was surrounded by Prussia Street, Aughrim Street and the North Circular Road. In 1954, cattle would be herded on foot from the farms of County Dublin, sharing the roads with the few cars. Pigs and sheep were also sold. Sales were generally held every Wednesday, when the mobile banks arrived. Livestock salesmen had cattle lairs in the vicinity, such as Craigie Bros, Gavin Lowe, Ganly & Sons.

On the 15th October, 1954 (Friday), the sheep sale was at 12.30, disposing of 3,000 sheep (Galway Cross-Bred, Cheviot and BF Horned Ewes, and a number of rams). In December, 400 cattle were sold at the Fat Stock Show & Sale.

Dublin Corporation's Abattoir and Dead Meat Market, was nearby at 121 North Circular Road (just after Blackhorse Avenue, behind red-brick houses), and included a special "kosher section" for Jews.

The charming and imposing red-bricked South City Markets in South Great Georges Street, were in fact a collection of shops, with offices and flats on the upper floors.

Grocery

Before the coming of supermarkets in the 1960's, there were hundreds of small shops around Dublin, such as general grocers, butchers, bakers, greengrocer, etc. People shopped daily in their local shops, but the heavy items could be delivered free by the shop's own messenger boy. In 1954, there was no self-service in even the big grocery shops, and customers lined up at counters to be served by the shop assistant (who usually wore a white or brown light overcoat). Big slabs of butter, cheese, and processed meat were cut into small portions by the assistant. Loose biscuits and other products such as tea-leaves were weighed to your requirements. Your own shopping bag was then filled, or you could have the groceries delivered by the shop. Messenger boys employed by shops rode bicycles around town and suburbs, fitted with big wire baskets on the front, delivering peoples "messages" (groceries). The "Messenger Boys Derby" was held in the Phoenix Park in August, with the lads riding their employer's bikes.

Alex Findlater was the supremo of the grocery shop, with his biggest shop in 28-32 Upper O'Connell Street, and 20 other branches in the suburbs, from Bray to Malahide.

H. Williams had twelve grocery shops around Dublin, including 45/47 Henry Street, and even a shop at 25 The Rise in Mount Merrion. They successfully evolved into supermarkets in the 1960's.

Liptons had nine shops around Dublin, including 60 Dame Street, and 101 Parnell Street.

Home & Colonial Tea Stores was another grocery chain, with seven branches, namely 15 North Earl Street, 14 Moore Street, 40

Georges Street South, 46 Upper Camden Street, 193 Lower Rathmines Road, Dun Laoire, and Bray.

The Blanchardstown Mills was in fact a grocery-shop chain, with eight outlets, including 119-122 Thomas Street (Headquarters).

Dunnes Stores was in its infancy, with stores only in Patrick Street in Cork, and O'Connell Street in Limerick.

Leverett and Frye was the "bees-knees" of upmarket grocers, with shops in Grafton Street, Sandymount, Rathgar, Dundrum, and Stillorgan. In February, they opened a gourmet shop upstairs in 36 Grafton Street, with seating for exclusive customers.

Robert Smyth & Sons, 6/7 St Stephens Green (near Grafton Street), for decades advertised themselves simply as "Smyths of the Green", being exclusive grocers and wine merchants.

W & A Gilbey, 46/47 O'Connell Street Upper, were important wine merchants, with over two dozen branches around the city, including 206 Harold's Cross Road (opposite Cooneys grocers). Their "bonded" wine stores were in the big stone arches under Harcourt Street Railway Station.

There was no shortage of bread shops, since all the big bakeries had many small retail outlets, including Bolands, Kennedy, Joseph Downes, and Johnston Mooney & O'Brien.

The Tea Time Express, 51b Dawson Street, was famous for its cakes, and their small shop also operated as lunch and tea rooms.

The Irish Yeast Company, 6 College Street, were suppliers to home cooks, especially for wedding-cake decorations.

Dublin was riddled with useless turf-accountants shops, otherwise known as Bookmakers (Bookies), and they had nothing to do with fuel for your fire, or your tax affairs, nor books. They were gambling dens, initially for wasting your housekeeping money on horse races ("the turf"), and then included greyhound dog racing, and nowadays football matches. P.J. Kilmartin was the biggest company, and had shops in most streets and neighbourhoods. Mirrelson only had a few branches.

Greenes Bookshop & Post Office in Clare Street only recently closed.

Bustling O'Connell Street in the 1950's, with Clerys clock on the right.

Junction of Dame Street and South Great Georges Street. The corner premises was built by Burtons Menswear in 1920. The famous Pims Department Store was replaced by a dreadful office block on the left side of this recent photo.

Findlaters Grocery Stores had branches all over Dublin, most sporting an external triangular clock. Clockwise from top left: Dun Laoghaire, Upper Baggot Street, Dalkey, Blackrock, Rathmines, Howth. (Courtesy of Alex Findlater).

This quaint shop in College Street, beloved of cake-makers, only recently closed.

Entertainment

St Patrick's Day

The biggest public event of the year occurred on 17th March, St Patricks Day, when a lively and colourful Parade wound its way through Dublin city centre (and other Parades were held all over Ireland).

People wore a sprig (or even a small bunch) of real green shamrock in their lapels, but only if it had been blessed in the church. The Post Offices did a roaring trade in tiny parcels and special plastic envelopes, containing blessed shamrock, posted to all corners of the world.

The Blessing of Shamrock took place at Collins Barracks at 9.30, when all the soldiers received sprigs of blessed shamrock from Fr John O'Regan, and then paraded around the square. There was Open-air Mass outside St Patrick's Garrison Church at Cathal Brugha Barracks (Grove Road/Harold's Cross) and also in Clancy Barracks (Islandbridge).

The Irish Times had a listing for the Irish Industrial and Cultural Parade, including the following information. The parade started at 11.30 am in St Stephens Green, went down Dawson Street, Nassau Street, Lower Grafton Street, Westmoreland Street, O'Connell Street (west side), around Parnell Square, and back down the east side of O'Connell Street. There were seven sections, each led by a Marshall.

Section 1 was headed by a Colour Party of IRA members, and comprised the Irish Transport & General Workers Union Band, Connrad na Gaedilge, Clann na h-Eireann, Friends of the Irish Language, Cara, Cumann Brisead na Teorann (Anti-Partition), Eire og School of Dancing, Knights of Malta, Glasthule School of Dancing, Cumann na bPiobaire Uileann, Masque Theatre Group, Theatre Cinema Association, Bundoran Development Association, Newspapers, ESB, Bord na Mona, Solas Teo, Dublin Gas Company.

Section 2 included Fintan Lalor Pipe Band, Guinness, Power, Jameson, Mountjoy Brewery, Cairnes (Drogheda brewery), Perry, Mineral Waters Distributors, Schweppes, Pepsi Cola, Mervue Dairy, Lucan

Dairy. Section 3 included City of Dublin Girls Pipe Band, Mitchelstown Creameries, Sugar Company, Urney Chocolates, Bolands Bread, Clover Meats, Gateaux Cakes, Castlebar Bacon Company, Lorcan O'Toole Band, Fry-Cadbury, Johnston Mooney bread, Associated Chocolate, Mackintosh, Lemons Pure Sweets, Williams & Woods, Chef Products, Chocolate Tobler, F. H. Steele & Co, Henry Denny, Redbreast Preserving Co, Chivers, Canned Products, Emerald Girls Pipers Band. Section 4 included P. J. Carroll, Malone Bros, Crean & Son, Ashtown Tin Box Co, Marie Jeanne flowers, Erins Own Household Products, Irish Coopers & Packages, Mitchell & Son, Aspro. Section 5 included Prescotts Dye Works, Gaeltarra Eireann, C & R. Barnes, Eirecol Cotton, Bradmola (hosiery), Burrows. Section 6 had Glasthule Pipers Band, CIE, G.N.R, Irish Dunlop Ltd, Greenmount Oil Co (Harold's Cross), Ryan Self-Drive, Messenger Service, LEP Transport, W.F. Poole & Co, Irish Multiwheel, F.P. Sarre, St Agnes Boys Brass & Reed Band, Aer Lingus, Ford (Archer, Autocars, Walden, Smithfield), E. Cullen & Son. The last section comprised Eire Nua, Cement Ltd, Flemings Fireclay, Brooks Thomas, Baxendale & Co, Tedcastle McCormack, J and C McLoughlin, Donald McFearson, James Ryan & Co, F.P. Sarre, Gallagher Furlong & Roarty, Gowna Wood industries.

St Patrick's Day in 1954 was a sunny day, with thousands up from rural Ireland for the matches in Croke Park (Gaelic football and hurling), Dalymount Park (soccer), and Lansdowne Road (rugby). The soccer and Gaelic matches were broadcast "live" on radio, except for the hurling match because of a dispute between the Gaelic Athletic Association (GAA) and Radio Eireann.

The Kennel Club Dog Show was held in the Royal Dublin Society (RDS) in Ballsbridge, with 1,100 dogs entered, and the best dog was an Irish Wolfhound brought over from England.

There was Horse-racing at Baldoyle, near Howth, with special buses from Eden Quay in the city centre.

The Zoo was packed that day, and numerous cyclists headed to the mountains and sea for relaxation. Two special trains carried 800 day-trippers to Belfast.

"An Tostal"

"An Tostal" festival was held around Ireland, from 18th April to 9th May, as a celebration of all things "Irish", having been initiated in 1953. In 1954, the Opening ceremony was in O'Connell Street, with the President of Ireland and other dignitaries reviewing a parade from a temporary platform in front of the GPO. The parade lasted an hour, with a military display, 30 floats in a Festival of Flowers, and a pageant with costumed actors. There were also parades in other cities and towns around the country.

During the festival, "Donnybrook Fair" was re-enacted in the grounds of "Montrose", a private house in Donnybrook. There was a Fireworks Display in the "Fifteen Acres" in the Phoenix Park on 28th April, an International Folk Dancing Festival in the National Stadium on the South Circular Road (May 4th to 8th), a Floral Festival (floats of flowers) in Dun Laoire, ceilis in the Gresham Hotel and the Mansion House, music and dancing in the Phoenix Park, including bands and choirs. There were coach tours in and around Dublin for visitors. The Four Courts building was floodlit on the outside, and presumably other public buildings.

The symbol of "An Tostal" was a modern "work-of-art", called the "Bowl of Light", in the centre of O'Connell Bridge, erected for the first Tostal in 1953. Many Dubliners did not like it, and hence the nickname "The Thing". It comprised a big copper bowl and plastic flames, on an arched tubular metal support, over a pool of water, probably about 10 feet high in total. An irate Trinity College student threw the "flames" into the River Liffey in the last week of April, 1953, but not even a dive in April 1955 could recover them, because the water was too murky and dark. The Lord Mayor erected a giant candle in front of the Mansion House in 1953, but that was also vandalised.

Spring Show, and Horse Show

The Spring Show & Industries Fair, was held in the RDS, Ballsbridge, from the 4th-8th May, with 400 trade stands. Because it was primarily aimed at farmers, it included pony jumping, dressage displays, cattle sales, and numerous competitions for bulls, sheep, pigs, dairy produce, and poultry. Trade stands included, Carrolls cigarettes, James Hicks & Sons of Pembroke Street (handmade furniture), James Weldon of Clarendon Street (silverware), Jacobs biscuits, Rowans (garden seeds), Hammond Lane Foundry (kitchen ranges), Lamb Bros (Fruitfield marmalade), Slowey of Henry Street (ladies fashions), Lenehans of Capel Street (new combine harvester), McGee of Ardee (combine harvester), Mc Kenzie of Pearse Street (farm machinery), Thompson of Abbey Street (farm machinery), and Pye radios. Todd, Burns department store had a real bungalow, displaying curtains and carpets, which furnishings could be purchased with the aid of 3-year Hire Purchase (HP).

The very fashionable Dublin Horse Show was held in the RDS in early August, and the British show-jumping team won the Aga Khan Trophy. Miss Iris Kellett entered seven of her own horses (she had a riding stables where Mespil Estate was being built beside Leeson Street Bridge). The Army No 1, No 2 and No 3 Bands played every day that week. The Horse Show was similar to the Spring Show, with hundreds of trade stands, and ancillary entertainment. During Horse Show Week, there were 1,200 entries for the Flower Show in Pembroke Hall of the RDS, organised by the Royal Horticultural & Aboricultural Society.

Mansion House Shows & Exhibitions

Although the RDS in Ballsbridge was the venue for big exhibitions and shows, the Mansion House (actually the big Round Room, and also the Supper Room) in Dawson Street was more accessible with public transport, and as usual, there was a full programme of events during 1954, the following being some of the highlights. In January, the 12th annual Bird Show, organised by the Irish Fur & Feather Association, attracted 950 entries, including racing pigeons, budgies, canaries, and furry rabbits. The Ramsey Perpetual Memorial Trophy was won by a Yorkshire canary.

February saw the RGDATA exhibition (retail grocery trade). In April, there were 700 entries for the Flower Show, organised by the Royal Horticultural Society. In June, the Midsummer Fair was held, in aid of the Adelaide Hospital, including a Siamese Cat Show, with 70 entries, and a Fashion Parade by the Norma Griffin Academy (not on the same catwalk!). In July, the 2nd Irish Drapery Trade Fair & Fashion Parade was open to the trade and the public.

The Ideal Homes Exhibition was the big event in September, with 2/- admission charge. The 50 stands included displays of electric cookers and washing machines. A big marquee on the rear lawn, was the venue for the Betty Whelan Fashion Display. Norman Metcalfe gave a recital on the Hammond Organ (Spinet model), displayed by Pigott & Co. Irish Estates had a display of a typical furnished livingroom from their flats-to-let complex in Mespil Road/Sussex Road, including furniture by William Hicks. September was also the month for the Royal Horticultural Society Autumn Show.

In October, the Irish Dachshund Club's 22nd Annual show took place. November saw the Indian League gala dance and cultural show.

Nowadays, the Mansion House is still the Lord Mayor's residence, the Supper Room is "Fire" restaurant, and the Round Room is reserved for occasional big gatherings.

Other Shows & Exhibitions

Besides the big shows, the RDS organised smaller events throughout the year, including bloodstock (horses) sales in February, the Bull Show in March (966 bulls entered), and the Irish Kennel Club Show (dogs) also in March.

The Burton Hall in Stillorgan organised regular indoor horse-jumping and displays, and also the "Tostal" Dog Show in April.

In October, the Dublin Cocker Society held their Annual Show in the Damer School on St Stephens Green.

In December, there were 900 entries for the 26th Championship of the Dublin Dog Show Society in Cathal Brugha Army Barracks in Rathmines (prior to 1952 was called Portobello Barracks).

The larger hotels had ballrooms and lecture halls, which were often used for public events. The Aberdeen Hall in the Gresham Hotel was the venue for the 5th annual NAIDA Fashion Parade. November was French wine week in Dublin, and a written examination on production, handling and serving of French wine was held in the Royal Hibernian Hotel, and also in the Gas Company Theatre in D'Olier Street. In July, the 11th Annual Exhibition of Malahide Horticultural Society took place in the Grand Hotel Ballroom.

The Shankill Model Flying Club competition took place in Bray, using model airplanes with engines. Another popular event during the year was the Model Aircraft Exhibition in the Mansion House. And in September, there was a model airplane competition in Baldonnel Airport.

In March, the CMS Hall (Hibernian Church Missionary Society – Protestant), 35 Molesworth Street, was the venue for the Rose Show and Decorative Floral Exhibition.

In June, the Royal Horticultural Society Flower Show was held in the Metropolitan Hall, Lower Abbey Street, while in November, there were 400 entries in the National Chrysanthemum Society show in the same hall.

In November, the Photographic Society of Ireland centenary exhibition took place in Dawson Hall.

The Olympia Theatre, and the National Stadium, were used for occasional Ice Skating Shows.

Music & Concerts

In January, Our Lady's Choral Society and the Radio Eireann (RE) Symphony Orchestra performed "Elijah" in the National Stadium on the South Circular Road. This orchestra also used the Phoenix Hall in Exchequer Street (Dame Court) for broadcasting their public concerts, and availed of the big organ in this venue. 700-800 children often attended Tuesday morning concerts and short talks about music in this Hall. On the 27th September, the Capitol Theatre was the venue for a performance by Our Ladys Choral Society with the RE Symphony Orchestra of "Dream of Gerontius" by Elgar. This orchestra was also in the Gaiety Theatre for the official opening concert of the Sunday Promenade series, on the 18th October.

Other events in January included the Swords "Mummers" performing at Sluagh Hall, Swords, and St Gabriels Boys Club in Mount Argus, Harold's Cross, performing the musical, "Pirates of Penzance".

The UCD Musical Society staged a concert in Aula Maxima, Newman House, in March. This month was also the time for the Pipe Band Competition, Oireachtas na Rince, and the Ulster Girls Choir, all in the Mansion House.

"Immanuel" a biblical play by C. Logan Wright, was performed in Christchurch Cathedral, on 9th April. The Hibernian Catch Club, a very old musical society/choir founded by Christchurch Cathedral, is still going strong.

During the year, "The Mikado" by Gilbert & Sullivan, was presented in the Rupert Guinness Hall, by St James Gate Musical Society (Guinness staff). William J. Watson gave an organ recital at St Annes Church, Dawson Street. A Grand Variety Concert was held in the Gresham Hotel, in aid of St Joseph of Cluny Foreign Missions (admission 3/0). The Catholic University Secondary School (CUS), Leeson Street, performed the Pirates of Penzance in their own theatre. The Archbishop Byrne Hall, 36-37 Harrington Street (home of the Catholic Girl Guides), was often used for concerts and shows. The ITGWU Band went to Holland for the International Music Festival (the modern Liberty Hall was not yet built).

In May, the 46th annual Feis took place in the Father Mathew Hall, Church Street. The Fr Mathew Players also put on plays during the year, and the pantomime "Cinderella" at Christmas.

Also in May, the Feis Ceol competitions took place in venues around Lower Abbey Street, including the Metropolitan Hall (now Irish Life/National Lottery), the Abbey Lecture Hall (probably beside the Ormond & Scots Presbyterian Church), and the CIE Club Hall in nearby Marlborough Street (Earl Place). The Metropolitan Hall was used as the venue for school choirs during the Feis Ceol.

To wrap up the year in December, the Pioneer Musical & Dramatic Society staged "Arabian Nights" in the St Francis Xavier Hall, Gardiner Street.

Museums & Galleries

The Chester Beatty Library was located on Shrewsbury Road in prosperous Ballsbridge, and the Arts Council was housed in adjacent Ailesbury Road (No 10). In January 1954, the Irish Independent newspaper contained a photo of Mr John A. Costello in the Arts Council building, presenting a portrait to Sir Alfred Chester Beatty, painted by Sean O'Sullivan.

It was a very fashionable occasion for the April opening of the 125th Royal Hibernian Academy (RHA) Exhibition in the National College of Art, which was located to the side of Dail Eireann, and behind the National Library. Artist, Sean Keating, was President of the RHA at that time, and there were 139 exhibits in the show. In August, the Exhibition of Living Art was held in the National College of Art.

In June 1954, the centenary of the birth (16/10/1854) of Oscar Wilde was marked by an exhibition in the Long Room of Trinity College Library. In October, 1954, a plaque was unveiled at 21 Westland Row, his birthplace. Oscar Wilde died in 1900.

In October, the Plunkett Centenary Exhibition was held in Pearse Street Library, in honour of Sir Horace Plunkett and the Co-Operative Movement. Also in October, there was an exhibition of paintings by Brother Joseph McNally FSC in the Little Theatre of Brown Thomas in Grafton Street.

During the year, there was an Exhibition of Indian Child Art at 8 Merrion Square, attended by General Mulcahy (Minister for Education), and also the Oireachtas Art Exhibition in the Municipal Art Gallery, Parnell Square.

Other Entertainment

The annual Military Parade took place on Easter Sunday, to celebrate the 1916 Easter Rising, right up to 1969, when "The Troubles" started in Northern Ireland. The parade went past the GPO in O'Connell Street, with huge crowds attending, and consisted of thousands of soldiers, sailors, airmen, Gardai, and numerous rousing bands, lorries, tanks, and guns. A few Air Corps planes flew over the city. For boys (young and old), the parade was a spectacular and memorable event, beating Cowboys & Indians games by a long shot.

After the parade, and obviously also throughout the year, a trip up to the top of the 134 feet high Nelsons Pillar in the centre of O'Connell Street was a big treat, affording wonderful views of Dublin, including the mountains and the sea. Alas, after being blown up in 1966 by both the IRA and then Dublin Corporation, Dublin lost a real tourist attraction.

The Dublin Zoo was, and still is, the biggest attraction for children of all ages. In the 1950's, the elephants could stretch their trunks across a moat, and accept snacks from childrens hands. Children could take unaccompanied jaunts around the Zoo on the backs of baby elephants. Every June, there was a formal Garden Party for invited guests, and later in the month, another party for invited children.

Although the Crowning of Our Lady (in May), and Corpus Christi (in June), were religious events, these street processions attracted thousands in all parishes throughout Ireland, and together with hymn-singing, flags and buntings, were as good as street carnivals.

James Joyce was a Dubliner (from Harold's Cross to be exact), and his most famous (although almost impossible to decipher) fictional creation was the book entitled "Ulysses", describing the wanderings of Leopold Bloom around Dublin on the 16th June 1904 (nicknamed Bloomsday thereafter). Despite the book being ignored for decades, the 50th anniversary of Bloomsday was celebrated by a handful of intellectuals, with a pilgrimage from the Martello Tower in Sandycove into the city centre. This tower had been derelict for years, and was sold in November, 1954.

Many people played "cards" at home, but group competitions were also popular, such as Bridge Competitions, and Whist Drives (nothing to do with a spin in the countryside!). There were Whist Drives in the Bernadette Hall, Redmonds Hill, Rathmines, every Monday & Thursday at 8.30pm, with a Score card costing 2/6, no prize less than 10/-, and £15 for the top score. Fullers Café, Grafton Street, held a Grand Whist Drive in aid of the Infantile Paralysis Fellowship, with a Score Card costing 2/6, and prize of 3 guineas for the top score. In January, there was a Bridge Competition in the Four Courts Hotel.

Hotels

The Gresham Hotel in O'Connell Street Upper was probably the best hotel in Dublin, if not in Ireland. Throughout the year, various groups held their annual ball or dance in the Gresham, for example, the Bon Secours Hospital held its first annual ball here, 400 staff attended the Aer Lingus Annual Dance here, and there was a Champagne Ball in aid of charity.

The Shelbourne Hotel in St Stephens Green was probably on a par with the Gresham Hotel. In February, the Federation of Irish Manufacturers had its annual general meeting (AGM) in the Shelbourne Hotel, followed by their annual dinner in Clerys restaurant. The 20th AGM of Arklow Pottery was held in the Shelbourne Hotel.

In April, 400 members attended the AGM of the Irish Countrywomens Association (ICA) in the Royal Hibernian Hotel, 48 Dawson Street. This hotel was in the same league as the Shelbourne and Gresham hotels, and featured the Buttery Cocktail Bar, and the Leinster Hall for banquets and dances. Nowadays the site is the modern offices of Davy Stockbrokers.

The Russell Hotel, 102-104 St Stephens Green, was another top hotel, but not so popular as the bigger competitors.

Jurys Hotel, at the corner of College Green and Anglesea Street, was very popular, especially for Wedding Breakfasts, long before big afternoon and evening feasts were introduced. Originally, this was the Prince of Wales Hotel, and is nowadays a modern office block. The O'Connell Schools Past Pupils Union held their annual dinner here. The nearby Moira Hotel, 15 Trinity Street, was small and well-respected, but was later demolished to make way for a multi-storey car park.

The Dolphin Hotel, 49 Essex Street, was popular with educational groups, for example, the annual dinner of St Flannans College PPU (Ennis), attended by the local Bishop, Rockwell College PPU dinner, Synge Street PPU dinner. This architecturally impressive building is now a District Court.

Wynn's Hotel in Lower Abbey Street, and the Clarence Hotel on 6,7,8 Wellington Quay, were popular with rural visitors. The Clarence also owned the Royal Exchange Temperance Hotel on 5/6 Parliament Street. In February, there was the annual dinner in the Clarence Hotel of the Dublin Cattle Salesmasters Association.

Other smaller hotels around the city centre included the Central, (Exchequer Street/Georges Street - above shops), Wicklow (6-8 Wicklow Street), Buswells (25,26,27 Molesworth Street), North Star (still at 26-30 Amiens Street), Great Northern (12-13 Amiens Street), Morans (Talbot Street - originally a Temperance Hotel), Mont Clare, (13/14 Clare Street), Grosvenor (5 Westland Row, right beside the railway bridge, but gone now), Powers (47 Kildare Street), Ormond (Ormond Quay), City Arms (54 Prussia Street, beside the Cattle Mart). In February, the Irish Commercial Travellers Association held their 37th Annual General Meeting in the Central Hotel.

The Swiss Chalet Hotel and Restaurant was on 2 Merrion Row. Every Sunday night they held a Ceili and Old Time Dance, with the Fingal Ceili Band. During the year, the Franciscan College PPU had their Grand Dance, from 8pm-12midnight, costing 3/-. Nowadays it is absorbed into the adjoining Shelbourne Hotel.

Out in the distant suburbs, there were fine hotels, such as Red Island Resort in Skerries, Grand Hotel in Malahide (which still has its ballroom), the Country Club in Portmarnock (the Fingal Harriers Hunt Ball was on the 31st December, from 9pm-3am), St Lawrence Hotel in Howth (faced the harbour, but now gone), Salthill Hotel in Monkstown (room and breakfast for 15/6. Reduced rates for permanent guests. Lunch is 5/6, dinner is 9/6. Lantern Bar), Royal Marine in Dun Laoghaire, Cliff Castle Hotel in Dalkey, Royal Starlight Hotel in Bray, Grand Hotel in Greystones, and Osberstown House in Naas (owned by Lawlors, and had hot and cold water in all rooms).

Ballrooms

Most of the big hotels in Dublin had ballrooms, in which annual staff dances and dinner-dances were held, amongst other events. There were many Hunt Balls in the hotels during Horse Show Week. All the ballrooms had resident orchestras, or sometimes visiting bands, performing waltzes, foxtrots, etc.

There were very popular ballrooms also in Clerys Department Store, Metropole Cinema, Savoy Cinema etc.

The famous and hugely popular Metropole in Lower O'Connell Street comprised a cinema, Adam Room for cocktails, Silver Grill restaurant, Tostal Room, Odeon Suites, and Georgian Room for dancing and cabaret. Friday night dancing was from 9pm to 1am, for 5/-, and the Saturday Matinee dance was from 3pm to 6pm, costing 2/6. The Golden Jubilee Ball of St Johns Ambulance Brigade was held in the Metropole Ballroom. Sadly, the city planners allowed this wonderful emporium to be demolished in the 1970's to make way for British Home Stores, and the plain modern building is now occupied by Penneys Department Store.

Clerys Ballroom was on an upper floor of the department store. In the middle of October 1954, the Passionist priests in Mount Argus organised an informal dance in aid of their African Missions in Bochanaland, with the Billy Watsons Orchestra (9pm to 1am for 5/-, with spot prizes). Dockrells staff dance was held in Clerys Ballroom in January 1954.

The Four Provinces, 46-48 Harcourt Street, was a very popular stand-alone ballroom (later became the TV Club with Eamon Andrews). In the middle of October, there was a Medical Students Dance from 9pm to 1am, for 3/6, with spot prizes, featuring Pat Moran & His Orchestra.

The National Ballroom, 20/21 Parnell Square North, was an institution, much favoured by rural people living in Dublin. Dancing was from 8pm to midnight, 3/6, with Spots. The Ierne Sports & Social Club, 12 Parnell Square, was also popular with country people. Club 31, Ancient Order of Hibernians (AOH), 31 Parnell Square, also held dances.

The Crystal Ballroom, 21a South Anne Street, held a dance for the Irish Nurses Organisation in the middle of October, from 8pm to midnight, for 3/6, with spots. The Olympic, 17-19 Pleasants Street, off Camden Street, was well known to rural dancers.

Smaller venues also organised dancing, such as the CIE Club in 98-100 Marlborough Street, Brugh an Airm in 1 Parnell Square,

Embassy in 19a/20 Dorset St Upper and 3 Granby Lane, and CYMS in Harrington Street. The Tramps Ball, sponsored by An Oige, was held in the Mansion House in October.

The Top Hat Ballroom in Dun Laoire, and the Arcadia Ballroom in Bray, were popular with dancers from all quarters.

Restaurants

Obviously, all the big hotels had good restaurants, and most of the large department stores also had cafes or restaurants, notably Clerys. The latter was also popular for company dinners and public events. For example, there was a newspaper photo of New Ireland Assurance Company (of 12 Dawson Street) making a staff presentation in Clerys Restaurant. The actor, William Bill Boyd, who played "Hopalong Cassidy" in numerous cowboy films, was guest of honour at a Variety Club of Ireland lunch in Clerys Restaurant during the year.

The Metropole, 35-39 O'Connell Street Lower, besides its famous ballroom and cinema, had a popular restaurant, where a 3-course Christmas dinner could be had for 12/6 in 1954. The Savoy cinema, 16-19 Upper O'Connell Street, also had a fine restaurant.

The Red Bank, 19/20 D'Olier Street and backing on to 3/4 Hawkins Street, was famous as a fish restaurant for many decades, since it was originally Burton Bindons Restaurant. In 1970 it was converted into the Blessed Sacrament Chapel, and is now Ashfield Hostel.

In the 1950's, Louis Jammett was a famous French restaurant on 46 Nassau Street (with full-height elaborate bay window), extending into 1,2,3 Adam Court off Grafton Street. The rear part of the extensive premises was the Harp Music Hall in Adam Court in 1893, then the Harp Tavern in 1899, with McEntaggart's Empire Restaurant in the Dawson Street part that same year. It became Kidds Restaurant in 1923, and then Jammets shortly afterwards. The restaurant closed in 1967 and became the Berni Inn pub in the 1970's, while the rear section was Lillies Bordello nightclub for many years.

Mitchells, 9-11 Grafton Street, was an upmarket establishment, comprising restaurant, café, and confectionary (cake) shop - the Blue Peter Sherry & Snack Bar was in No 11. The premises had been rebuilt in 1928 by G & T Crampton, and sported an impressive facade. Nowadays McDonalds hamburgers operate a fast-food cafe in the same building.

DBC Tea Rooms, 37/38 St Stephens Green, was actually a fashionable restaurant operated by the Dublin Bread Company. McConnells Advertising Agency held their annual staff dinner here in December 1954.

Other nice eateries around Dublin included the Unicorn at 11 Merrion Row (Italian food), Paradiso at 31-32 Westmoreland Street (below the Irish Times offices), Bernie's Café at O'Connell Bridge, Sheries Restaurant at 3 Lower Abbey Street (still trading), and the Green Tureen at 95 Harcourt Street (which was associated with a famous murder trial). More modest fare could be obtained in Burdock Fish Saloon at 2 Werburgh Street (still a great Fish & Chips take-away), and Cafollas Ice Cream parlours at 8/9 Lower O'Connell Street (Broadway Cafe), and 47/48 Lower O'Connell Street.

The three Bewleys Cafés were a Dublin institution, which was officially founded as tea and coffee importers in 1840 by the Bewley family, Quakers, although they had already imported tea from China in 1835. Their first café opened in 1894 in 13 South Great Georges Street (later included 12), then 10/12 Westmoreland Street opened in 1896, and finally 78/79 Grafton Street opened in 1927 in two existing buildings (in 1893, 79 was five-storey, and 78 was four-storey). 94-96 Middle Abbey Street was their tea & wine merchant shop. Bewleys always had a coffee-bean roaster in the café window, which was topped up by a worker in white overalls, and coffee aromas wafted out the window vent to draw customers in.

The Beaufield Mews coffee shop in distant Stillorgan was advertising its Winter Opening Hours from 1st October, being Tuesday & Thursday only from 8pm to 10.30pm, for coffee and savouries. By 1960, the coffee shop had matured into a restaurant, which went on to achieve great fame for hungry families on Sunday afternoons.

Dublin Airport had a glamorous restaurant, which was frequented by car-owning patrons seeking a good night out. There were also Saturday night Dinner Dances, from 8pm to midnight, for 14/6, including a lovely meal. Throughout the day, the public could spend hours admiring the planes (and wealthy passengers) from the open-air viewing balconies and from the flat roof.

Dublin had many private (members-only) clubs in 1954, which had restaurants and bars, such as the Catholic Commercial Club (42 Upper O'Connell Street), Hibernian United Services Club (8 St Stephens Green), St Stephens Green Club (9 St Stephens Green), Dublin University Club/Trinity College (17 St Stephens Green), Irish Bankers Club (93 St Stephens Green), Kildare Street Club (1,2,3 Kildare Street - now Alliance Francaise), United Arts Club (3 Fitzwilliam Street Upper), Irish Rotary Club (12 Westmoreland Street).

Public Houses

Dublin was awash with pubs in 1954, although most were small and fairly basic, especially in the suburbs. All were "men-only" bars, with no lounges for relaxing. Stale beer and tobacco smells permeated the atmosphere. Many had been grocers shops in previous decades, with a counter (bar) on one side serving small bottles of porter, before the introduction of cold beer-cellars and pumps. Even when pint glasses of beer became the norm, half-pints were also popular. There were no "off-licences", but sometimes at closing time, a drinker could get some extra drink to take home in a brown paper bag (hiding bottles).

One of the most famous pubs in the city was "The Irish House" (O'Meara) on Wood Quay, at the corner of Winetavern Street, mostly because of its elaborate and colourful facades.

Downeys pub at 108 Upper Georges Street, Dun Laoire, re-opened in November 1953 when the owner died, after being picketed by the unhappy staff for 14 years!

Theatre

Theatre Royal
The gigantic Theatre Royal (often listed as The Royal), occupying the corner of Hawkins Street and Poolbeg Street, was a fantastic and

hugely popular entertainment venue, because a night out at "the pictures" comprised a film, plus a Variety Show. The resident orchestra was led by Jimmy Campbell, while Tommy Dando manned the organ, and a troupe of beautiful Royalette dancers added a touch of glamour.

This famous theatre was shown on the 1837 Ordnance Survey map, and later maps also refer to it as Leinster Hall, and it was rebuilt as the New Theatre Royal & Opera House (architect Frank Matcham) in 1897 using part of Leinster Hall. The premises was again completely rebuilt in 1935, then closed and demolished in 1962, to make way for the 1963 ugly office block called Hawkins House. The Department of Health wasted a fortune leasing the offices for nearly six decades, before it was demolished in 2020 by the private owner.

Normally, the film had three showings, 3pm, 6pm, and 9pm, and the variety show was at 4.45pm and 7.45pm. Sometimes, the film was replaced by a special celebrity, but there was always a variety show as well. Prices for the evenings entertainment ranged from 3/6, 7/6, 8/6, 10/-, and occasionally up to 21/-. Famous personalities who appeared during 1954 included Roy Rogers (King of the Cowboys), Nat King Cole, actress Vivian Blaine (of Guys & Dolls fame), singer Guy Mitchell, singer Lena Horne (with Teddy Fosters orchestra from England), singer Gracie Fields, pianist Arthur Rubenstein, and Mantovani with his wonderful orchestra.

The Christmas Variety Show in 1954 was called, "Christmas Crackers", featuring comedian Jack Cruise, Four Ramblers (vocal quartet), Royal Oultons, and Tommy Dando on the house organ.

The Theatre Royal could hold a few thousand people, so it was chosen for a Pioneer Rally in November (abstinence from alcohol).

Gaiety Theatre

In February, the Promenade Concerts (Proms) with the Radio Eireann Orchestra, were held in the Gaiety Theatre, 46-50 South King Street.

The Easter puppet show was mounted by the Teatro Podrecca Piccoli from Italy, comprising 1,200 marionettes (4-feet high figures), 40 artists, and 2,000 costumes.

In July, the famous D'Oyly Carte Opera Company performed in The Gondoliers.

In mid-October, the three-act play entitled "Seven Year Itch", was performed nightly at 8pm, and a Saturday matinee at 2.30pm, with prices of 7/6d, 5/-, 3/-, 1/-.

In November and December, the Dublin Grand Opera Society performed such operas as "La Boheme", and "Aida".

The Christmas pantomime, "A Date with Laughter", included such stalwarts as Jimmy O'Dea, Danny Cummins, and Maureen Potter.

Olympia Theatre

This famous theatre at 72 Dame Street was called the Empire Palace Theatre in 1907, and the Olympia Palace Theatre in 1954. In mid-October, "No Escape" was on nightly at 8pm, plus Saturday matinee at 3pm, with prices of 10/-, and 7/6 in the stalls, and 8/6, 6/-, and 4/- in the circles.

Alec Guinness appeared in March in "The Prisoner", a new play by Brigid Boland. The Schools Drama League was also held in March. During the year, Noel Coward visited Dublin to supervise rehearsals for his play, "Blithe Spirit". In December, the Christmas pantomime was "Jack & the Beanstalk".

Abbey Theatre (and Queens Theatre)

The Queens Theatre at 208-210 Pearse Street was built in 1909, and mostly went in for cabaret. After the Abbey Theatre in Lower Abbey Street went on fire in July 1951, the Abbey relocated to the Queens Theatre until 1966, and the former Queens building was demolished in 1975 to make way for an office block (Aras an Phiarsaigh).

The Abbey Theatre was founded in Abbey Street Lower in 1904, and following a fire in 1951 was demolished in 1961, to be replaced by the present very plain building in 1966. One of the founders of the Abbey, Maud Gonne McBride, died in April 1953, aged 88. In December, 1954, the Golden Jubilee of the Abbey was celebrated with three small plays, attended by the President of Ireland. Afterwards in the Green Room, a giant barm-brack (current cake) was shared.

In both Spring and Autumn of 1954, the Abbey performance at 8pm on Monday, Wednesday, and Friday was "The Devil a Saint Would Be", with "Twenty Years A-Wooing" on Tuesday and Thursday.

Gate Theatre

Edward Hilton and Michael McLiammoir were the main actors in this venue, assisted by Lord Longford. In October 1954, "The Importance of Being Earnest" was the play at 8pm (and Saturday at 2.30pm).

Pike Theatre

The Pike Theatre Club, 18a Herbert Lane, was a tiny (held 66 patrons) fringe theatre, which operated from 1953 to 1964. The Herbert Lane Follies were in action in January 1954 at 10.45 each night – revue, with piano accompaniment. In September, La Boheme was performed by the Nelson Paines puppet company, while in November, "The Quare Fellow" by Brendan Behan was performed. "The Rose Tattoo" was performed in 1957, and was raided by the Gardai for alleged obscenity.

There were a number of small theatres scattered around the city, including the Dublin Gas Company Theatre in D'Olier Street and also in Dun Laoghaire (some plays by Globe Theatre). In January, in the Players Theatre, Trinity College, "All my Sons" by Arthur Miller, was performed. The Bernadette Players put on "No Mans Land" in December (3/- and 2/-) in the recently opened Marian Hall in Milltown. The Garrick Theatre, 15 Parnell Square East, opened only on Saturday & Sunday nights, and closed in the 1960's. In December, The Childrens Theatre presented "The Tinder Box" in the Royal Irish Academy of Music (RIAM) in Westland Row.

Christmas pantomimes and shows for 1954 included "Date with Laughter" (Jimmy O'Dea) in the Gaiety Theatre, "Jack and the Beanstalk" in the Olympia Theatre, "A Slipper for the Moon" (Michael MacLiammoir) in the Gate Theatre. In St Francis Xavier Hall in Gardiner Street, the Pioneer Musical & Dramatic Society put on "Arabian Nights", while in the Father Mathew Hall in Church Street, the Fr Mathew Players performed "Cinderella". The Garrick Theatre Club in Parnell Square put on "The Facts of Life".

In December, 1954, Sheridan House, 13 Northumberland Road, opened as a hostel for touring actors, and was run by Lord Longford and Lennox Robinson.

Cinema

Before the advent of Irish television in the 1960's, Dubliners flocked to the "pictures" at least once a week (the films changed every week), and got very good value for their money. The reels never stopped rolling during the afternoons and evenings, and patrons could join a film at any time, and even stay to watch the whole show over again. The entertainment consisted of a feature film, and a secondary film, in addition to Pathe News, and the "trailers" (previews) for next weeks films. Uniformed ushers and usherettes directed you to your seat, and at the intervals sold orange ice pops, and small tubs of ice-cream.

The city centre had many comfortable cinemas, and every suburb had a more modest cinema.

Films released in 1954 included: White Christmas, The Caine Mutiny, The Glenn Miller Story, On The Waterfront, Seven Brides for Seven Brothers, 20,000 Leagues Under The Sea, and Rear Window by Alfred Hitchcock, starring Grace Kelly and James Stewart.

The Ambassador Cinema, with a big Waterford crystal chandelier over the staircase, only opened in 1954, and was the Rotunda Picture Theatre and Dance Hall before that. However, it was built as the Round Room in 1764 as an extension to the Lying-In Hospital (Rotunda Maternity Hospital), for holding concerts to raise hospital funds. In October 1954, the feature film was Danny Kaye in "Knock on Wood", showing at 3.00, 4.26, 6.52, and 9.18 (Sunday at 3.30 & 8.00). Entrance charges were 3/6 and 2/6.

The Savoy, beside the Gresham Hotel, was showing "Hell & High Water" in October, at 2.00, 4.20, 6.40, 9.00.

The Carlton, 52-54 Upper O'Connell Street, was showing "Give a Girl a Break" at 2.00, 4.20, 6.40, 9.00 (and also "Arena"). Their restaurant stayed open until 11pm.

The Gala Film Premiere of "On the Waterfront", with Marlon Brando and Eve Marie Saint, was showing in the Capitol Theatre in Princess Street (behind the Metropole) at 2.10, 4.25, 6.40, 8.55, with admission charges of £1.1.0, 10/-, 5/-, 3/6d. Also showing was, "Drums of Tahiti".

The Metropole Cinema (just south of the GPO) was showing "Romeo & Juliet" at 12.35, 3.15, 5.50, 8.30. The combined site of the Capitol and Metropole is now Penneys Department Store.

The Adelphi Cinema, 98-101 Middle Abbey Street, was a big and fashionable cinema, and in October was showing "Calamity Jane" at 2.00, 4.21, 6.42, 9.03. Their café opened from 10.30am to 11pm.

The Adelphi hosted the Premiere of the Irish comedy, "Happy Ever After", on 7th August, 1954, with Susan Stephen and Yvonne Carlo (American) attending. Also in August, "Knights of the Round Table" was screened in the Adelphi, starring Ava Gardner (part of the film had been shot in Luttrellstown Castle, Clonsilla, County Dublin).

The Adelphi stage (after rolling up the film screen) was honoured to host performances by the "Beatles" on November 7th and 8th, 1963, and another famous British rock band, the Rolling Stones, in January 1965. Both events required a large Garda presence to control the screaming fans out on the street, mostly teenage girls. Nowadays, the former cinema façade frames the exit from Arnotts car park.

The Corinthian, 4-6 Eden Quay, just east of Mooneys pub, was showing "Face to Face" and "Jungle Cavalcade", with full programmes at 3.30, 6.15, and 9.00. The cinema originally had an ornate façade, and then a blank concrete façade towards the end of the 20th century.

The Astor, 7 Eden Quay (which opened in 1953) was showing "Paradine Case" at 2.05, 4.20, 6.35, 8.55, and also "Nutcracker" (ballet). The façade consisted of the two red-bricked buildings, and looked small beside the Corinthian cinema next door.

Other north city centre cinemas in 1954 included the New Electric Cinema, 42-45 Talbot Street (which later became the Eblana Cinema), Plaza Picture Theatre, 22 Dorset Street Upper (corner of Granby Row), and Mary Street Cinema (12,13, Mary Street, with part in 39-40 Wolfe Tone Street).

The Regal Rooms, Hawkins Street, on the right-hand side of the much larger Theatre Royal, was showing "Ricochet Romance" at 2.05, 5.00, 7.55, and "Up to his Neck" at 3.22, 6.17, 9.12. Nearby was the Palace Cinema at 42 Pearse Street, which later became the Academy Cinema.

The Grafton, 72 Grafton Street, was showing "Waterloo Bridge" at 2.00, 4.15, 6.30, 8.45. Their restaurant operated from 10am to 9pm. Within a few years, the Grafton became a childrens paradise, showing only cartoons all day long. The Cameo, 43 Grafton Street, was showing "Laurel & Hardy" in 1951, but then closed in the face of competition from The Grafton.

The Green, 127 St Stephens Green, was showing "Please believe Me" at 4.05, 6.45, 9.20, plus "East of Sumatra". In the 1970's, the site became the Dandelion open-air market with stalls selling cheap goods, and then the Stephens Green Shopping Centre was erected on the whole block.

Other southside small cinemas included the Theatre de Luxe, 85-86 Lower Camden Street, the Stella and also the Princess in Rathmines, and the Tivoli, 135-138 Francis Street (became a theatre towards the end of the 20th century).

The Kenilworth cinema in Harold's Cross, was showing "Johnny Guitar" plus "Call of the Forest" with full programmes at 6.20 and 8.40 (Saturday matinees from 3.00), while the Classic in Terenure was showing "Since You Went Away" at 5.30 and 8.20.

Some scenes from "Captain Lightfoot" were filmed (shot) in Powerscourt, Enniskerry, starring Rock Hudson and Barbara Rush. The Irish actress, Louise Studley, also starred in this film.

The Phoenix Park Racecourse was recently re-developed as a housing estate.

The famous Theatre Royal was on Hawkins Street, with the tiny Regal cinema just visible on the right. (Courtesy of Dublin City Library & Archives).

The second building from the corner was the Grafton Cinema, and now a shop. The three-castles plaque in the centre of the bay window, is the crest for Dublin City.

A typical "eight" rowing boat, seen recently on the River Liffey at Islandbridge, and probably not unlike those used in the 1950's.

Sport

Badminton

In January, the "Dublin versus Derry" badminton match took place in the Dublin Gas Company Hall, D'Olier Street. The Pembroke versus Ailesbury match took place in Camden Row (probably in the Hall attached to the Protestant Home of Rest for the Dying at No 20). In April, 1954, a new Badminton Hall was opened in Whitehall Road, Kimmage, which is still going strong.

Boxing

In April, Scottish boxers were in action in the National Boxing Stadium on the South Circular Road, headquarters of the Irish Army Boxing Club. They were competing for the Kuttner Shield, and Ireland won by 7 matches to 3. In September, Ireland beat the Welsh boxing team, 6-4, in the same venue.

In May 1954, the German boxing team and Munich folk dancers visited the Lord Mayor of Dublin in the Mansion House. Later they competed in the sports hall of the Mental Hospital in Portlaoise. In October, the German boxing team beat Ireland 8-2 in the National Boxing Stadium.

In June, the Crumlin Boxing Club set off to Germany from Westland Row Railway Station, catching the Mail Boat from Dun Laoghaire to Holyhead in England, and a long journey afterwards.

Car Racing

The vast Phoenix Park was the venue for regular motorcar races. Also, in June, there were 51 entries in the Vintage Car Race on the Naas

Road (long before the dual-carriageway was built). Stock-car racing was introduced to Ireland in the Summer of 1954, with an event in August in Shelbourne Park greyhound track, Ringsend.

Cycle Racing

The 7-day Cycling Tour of Ireland, sponsored by An Tostal, was held in April. Shay Elliott of Ireland came second, behind the British winner, Bernard Pusey. Of the 108 riders who started in Dublin, only 15 returned, many having dropped out due to the gruelling weather.

An Ras Tailteann bicycle race was held from 1st to 8th August, starting from O'Connell Street in Dublin, cycling all over the island, including Northern Ireland, and finishing in the Phoenix Park, Dublin. It was won by nineteen year old Joseph O'Brien of the National Cycling Club.

The County Dublin Road Club held its annual Rollers Racing Contest in November in Dun Laoire Town Hall. Bikes were fixed to rollers, pedalled like mad, and the speeds were recorded on attached dials. Nowadays, people do this in expensive gyms.

Gaelic Football and Hurling

Croke Park in 1954 was very basic, with only one partially enclosed stand. The Artane Boys Band (from the notorious Industrial School for young orphan boys run by the Christian Brothers) always performed for the big matches.

Meath beat Kerry in the All-Ireland Senior Football Final on the 27th September 1954, 1 goal 13 points to 1 goal 7 points. Paddy O'Brien of Meath was named Sports Star of the week in the Irish Independent. In the senior hurling, Cork beat Wexford, 1-9 to 1-6, before a crowd of 85,000.

On the 21st November, 1954, in Croke Park, "Bloody Sunday 1920", was commemorated prior to the match between Wexford and Kildare. During the charity football match between Dublin and

Tipperary in November 1920, at the height of the War of Independence, the British Army, in a vicious, cowardly and murderous attack, opened fire on the innocent spectators (men, women, and children), killing fourteen, and wounding about sixty. Three innocent children, aged 10, 11 and 14, (one watching the match from the top of a boundary wall, and another sitting in a tree) were shot dead. Michael Hogan from Tipperary, was the only player to be killed, and the GAA later named a stand in his memory. With the bullet, the bayonet, and belligerent bullies, no wonder the British empire flourished prior to the age of democracy! In 1954, survivors and relatives were led onto the pitch in front of "Hill 16", where a "Decade of the Rosary" was recited in Irish by Fr Walsh of St Saviours Church, Dominick Street, the "Last Post" was sounded by three buglers from the Artane Boys Band, and the Tricolour flag was hoisted up from half-mast. There was a two-minute silence, concluded by the Reveille.

Golf

In February, the Irish Open Amateur Championship was held in the Royal Dublin Golf Club on Bull Island in Dollymount. The new clubhouse was officially opened in August by Taoiseach, Mr Costello (the old one burned down in 1943).

Greyhound Racing

Greyhound dog racing and gambling took place at Harold's Cross Stadium (Tuesday, Thursday, Friday evenings in the Summer season) and in Shelbourne Park Stadium in Ringsend (Monday, Wednesday, Saturday evenings).

Some people may remember another greyhound stadium in Chapelizod (Tuesday, Friday, Sunday), which had a short life on and off in the 1950's, but failed to obtain a licence. Entry to their Grand Stand was 3/6, and cheaper into the Popular Enclosure. It was then used for Speedway racing (scrambler motorbikes), midget car racing on

Sundays, and even held a wrestling tournament. The site is now the Chapelizod Industrial Estate.

Horseracing

The Irish Hospitals Sweepstake opposite the RDS in Ballsbridge was a Government-sponsored, but privately owned, lottery to raise funds to build hospitals, set up in 1930 as the Irish Hospitals Trust. The Sweep was based on the results of British horse-racing, such as the Grand National, Derby, and Cambridgeshire races. Such gambling was illegal in America and Britain (although not in Britain after 1950), but a huge black-market developed in these countries, and a few Irish businessmen made a fortune from the business.

Lucky Coady, 39 Dame Street, was selling tickets for the Sweep at £1 each, or shares at 10/-, 5/-, and 2/6d.

The Grand National Sweepstakes draw took place in Ballsbridge in January, when uniformed nurses picked the various potential winning tickets from a big revolving drum, and a full page of results was then printed in the daily newspapers. The actual race took place on the 27th March at Aintree, near Liverpool, and was won (by a neck) by Irish horse, Royal Tan, owned by Joe Griffin, trained by Vincent O'Brien, and Bryan Marshall was the jockey. On the 31st March, Royal Tan arrived by ship from Liverpool back in Dublin at the North Wall, and was paraded through Dublin, and even paid a visit to the Lord Mayor, Bernard Butler.

Horseracing in Dublin took place in the Phoenix Park Racecourse (Belvedere Plate in June), Leopardstown, and Baldoyle. Champion jockey, Gordon Richards, aged 50, retired in 1954.

Miscellaneous Sports

Polo was the preserve of wealthy horse-owners, and the Phoenix Park pitch is still used. On the 20th June, 1954, Nomads beat Quidnuncs, 3 to 1. That year also saw a spot of bicycle-polo in the Phoenix Park.

Rowing was generally the preserve of Dublin University (also known as Trinity College), and University College Dublin (also known as UCD), and long, shallow, narrow boats were used, called Eights because there were eight rowers in each, plus a cox in charge. June was the traditional time for the Trinity Regatta on the River Liffey at Islandbridge.

In November, Clonliffe Harriers (running and athletics) opened their new Stadium in Santry, which was later called Morton Stadium.

In June, there was a photo in the newspapers of the Catholic Boy Scouts on a camping weekend at Larch Hill in Rathfarnham, which included the 45th Dublin Troup (Mount Argus). The scouting HQ was at 71 St Stephens Green.

In June, the Royal St George Yacht Club held a regatta in Dun Laoire harbour. The following month, the nearby National Yacht Club opened a new slipway.

Roller skates (attached to your feet) were popular with youngsters, and even young adults. The Classic Roller Skating Rink, 22/23 Duke Street (behind The Curio shop, and beside Davy Byrne pub) was the place to socialise.

In 1954, the Dublin Maccabi Association (Jewish) opened their new Sports Ground and Clubhouse in Kimmage Road West. Nowadays, the Ben Dunne Gym occupies the site.

Rugby

On 9th January the New Zealand All Blacks (actually all white men) beat the Irish rugby team in Lansdowne Road Stadium, 14 points to 3 points. The All Blacks arrived in Amiens Street Train Station, and stayed in the Shelbourne Hotel. They practiced in College Park, inside Trinity College. Trains from all over Ireland brought the Irish rugby fans to Dublin. During the year, a new stand was built at Lansdowne Road.

Soccer

In November, the Republic of Ireland soccer team beat Norway, two goals to one goal, in Dalymount Park, Phibsborough. 34,000 attended, including President O'Kelly, Taoiseach Mr Costello, and Lord Mayor Alfie Byrne. The Football Association of Ireland (FAI) was founded in 1921, and was based in 80 Merrion Square.

Swimming

Tara Street Baths
Dublin Corporation owned the Wash-Houses & Pool at 18-22 Tara Street and 43/44 Poolbeg Street. The premises comprised a swimming pool with part gallery in the south half of the building. The centre section comprised the women's baths and wash houses plus drying chamber. The single-storey north portion was for the mens wash houses. The baths and wash-houses were probably used by poor people with no homes, or no bathroom in their homes. Charges in 1954 were as follows:

First Class Swimming Pond (Males Only): 10am to 7pm. 8d (boys 4d).
More expensive in Winter because the water was heated.
Second Class Swimming Pond: Half the foregoing prices.
Ladies Day: Monday, 3pm to 7pm.
Warm Reclining Baths : 1st class (Male & Female), 1s. 2nd Class 6d.

Iveagh Trust Public Baths, Bride Road, off Patrick Street
One swimming pond. 1pm to 7pm. Ladies Day is Tuesday. Adults 1s, children 6d. Nowadays, occupied by the Iveagh Fitness Club.
In November 1954, the Iveagh Baths was the venue for the Leinster Indoor Water Polo League.

The Turkish Baths in 8-14 Lincoln Place, near the Dental Hospital in the city centre, looked like an Muslim mosque. It closed by 1954, and was then used by Linco Services Ltd, dyers & cleaners.

Southside Sea Baths

Three venues: beside Blackrock Railway Station, Marine Parade in Dun Laoghaire, and Sandycove Point. The season ran from the 1st week of June to the last week of September, 8am to 8pm.

Adults 6d, children (under 16), 3d. Spectators 3d.

Separate dressing sections for males and females, but mixed bathing allowed.

Hot Reclining Baths in Dun Laoghaire, for most of the year: hot seawater (2/6), hot freshwater (2/-), Russian Steam Bath (4/-), seaweed bath (4/-), cold bath (1/-). Towels washed in laundry attached to the baths. Rest rooms and refreshment rooms.

Swimming and diving galas were frequent in Blackrock open-air sea baths.

The Forty Foot, Gentlemen Only, in Sandycove, was (still is) an open-sea free venue, but donations were accepted by the man on the gate.

Clontarf Baths Ltd, 123a Clontarf Road.

Cold swimming pool, 50 yards long and 33 yards wide, with male and females sections divided by a high wall. Adults 6d, children 4d. Hot seawater baths and seaweed baths, 2/6.

Water polo matches and swimming races every week.

Christmas Day swimming race for the Scully Cup.

Tennis

There were plenty of small Tennis Clubs around Dublin, including the Leinster Cricket Club in Rathmines. The Fitzwilliam Lawn Tennis Club at Wilton Place was the place to be seen, and in April, they hosted the Irish Open Hard Tennis Court Championship. Later, this club moved to Appian Way, off Leeson Street.

Radio

Radio Eireann

Ireland's national radio station was set up in the GPO in O'Connell Street in 1926, and was called 2RN, and then called Radio Eireann from 1937. There were also broadcasts from Cork from 1927. The erection of a transmitter in Athlone in 1933 improved reception in the midlands. Householders were required to have an annual radio licence from 1926 to 1972, after which a TV licence included the radio.

In 1954, Radio Eireann was on air from 8am to 9.30am, 1pm to 2.45pm, and 5.30pm until about 11.45pm.

Radio Eireann relied heavily on commercial sponsorship, and various companies were given a 15-minute slot for music and chat, to promote their image and products, usually including a catchy song or byeline. Sponsored programmes included, Emerald, Gala, Colgate Palmolive, Fry Cadbury, Prescotts, Birds, K & S, Crosse & Blackwell, Bradmola, Imco, Rowntree, Cotts of Kilcock, The Standard, Mackintosh, Keillers, Urneys, Donnelly, Gateaux, Fruitfield, Mitchelstown, Rowntree, Stork, Chivers, Ponds, Bachelors, Owens, Post Office Savings, and of course, Waltons at 2.30 on Saturday afternoons.

Popular Radio Eireann programmes in 1954 included "Musical Quiz" in April with Terry O'Sullivan (army team from Eastern Command won), "Take the Floor" with Din Joe (Denis Fitzgibbon) from 1953-1972, promoting ceili set-dancing, Paddy Crosbie (a National School teacher) with his charming "School Around the Corner", which started in 1954, and then transferred to Television from 1961-66. The hugely popular soap-opera "The Kennedys of Castleross", sponsored by Fry-Cadbury chocolate, hit the airwaves in April 1955, and lasted until 1973.

A week in the middle of January 1954 illustrates the fare on Radio Eireann:

Monday: News at 8am, Morning Music, Clar an Chomhchaidrimh, Colgate-Palmolive Programme, News, Signpost & Close Down at 9.30am. Fruitfield Programme at 1pm, Mitchelstown Programme, News & Topical Talk, "Radio Review" Programme, Rowntrees Programme, Birds Programme, Close Down at 2.30pm. Children at the Microphone at 5.30 pm (accompanied by Frances Coughlan on accordion, Thelma Byrne singing, Ursula Hough on violin, Veronica McSwiney on piano), Interlude at 5.57pm, Angelus, Out of Doors (with J. Ashton Freeman), Announcements (Stock Exchange prices, Signpost), News at 6.30pm, London Baroque Ensemble (records), Poetry Review (by Austin Clarke), The Music of Portugal (last of three programmes by Manuel Alves), Listen & Learn, Take the Floor (Din Joe invites you to his Ceili House, with the Garda Ceili Band), The Melody Lingers On (with Radio Eireann Light Orchestra, Radio Eireann Singers, soprano Renee Flynn, tenor Michael O'Duffy, Tommy Dando at the organ), Between The Bookends (James Plunkett reviews "Suite in Four Movements" by Eric Coates, and "Vaughan Williams" by Percy M. Young), Nuacht at 10pm, News at 10.15pm, Hospitals Trust Programme, City Newsreel, Magic Carpet (H.L. Morrow tells stories from the travellers, with music), Late Sports Results at 11.30, and closedown.

Tuesday: News at 8am, Gala Programme, Stork Margarine Programme, Chivers Programme, News, Signpost & Close Down at 9.30am. Fry-Cadbury Programme at 1pm, Donnellys Programme, News & Topical Talk, Birds Programme, Ponds Programme, Light Orchestral Music (records), and Close at 2.30pm. Lise (Irish drama) at 5.30pm, Interlude, Angelus, Sua-Amhranaiocht (Irish song), Rita Lynch Soprano (records), Announcements, News at 6.30pm, Blas Aduaidh, History Sings (introduced by Donagh MacDonagh, with Radio Eireann Singers), Whats On Your Mind (Macra na Feirme with Maxwell Sweeney), The Winter Proms (second half of concert in Gaiety Theatre, with Radio Eireann Symphony Orchestra), Country Journal (weekly magazine presented by Fred Desmond), Top of the Evening (by Kevin McCaul), Nuacht, News, Hospitals Trust Programme, Amhrain (Tomas O'Suilleabhain), The Nocturnes of John Field, Late Sports Results, and closedown.

Wednesday: News at 8am, Owens programme, Stork Margarine Programme, Post Office Savings Programme, News, Signpost, Close down at 9.30. Hospitals Requests at 1pm, News & Topical Talk, Hospitals Requests, and close at 2.30pm. Drawing & Painting (with Marion King) at 5.30pm, Music for Two Pianos (Mollie Phillips & Albert Healy), Interlude, Angelus, Pocus & Blip (story by Michael P. O'Connor), Cattle Market Report, News, Wednesday Recital (Bernadette & Vincent O'Neill on pianos, Egil Nordsjo, baritone), An Ghealluint nar Briseadh, Aris (drama), The Bowl of Light (discussion), Irish Dance Music (Andrew Keane on Uileann pipes), Fios Feasa Fonn, Farmers Forum (wth Michael Dillon), Nuacht, News, Hospitals Trust Programme, Mo Rogha Dem Shaothar Fein, Light Piano Music (Ita Flynn), Late Sports Results at 11.30pm and closedown.

Thursday: News at 8am, Emerald programme, Gala Programme, Colgate-Palmolive Programme, News, Signpost & Closedown at 9.30. Fry-Cadbury Programme at 1pm, Prescotts Programme, News & Topical talk, Birds Programme, "K & S" Programme, Crosse & Blackwell Programme, close at 2.30pm. Cogar A Leanie (Peadar O'Dubhda) at 5.30pm, Interlude, Angelus, The Little Girl Who Curtsied To The Owl (a story for children by Margaret Baker), Announcements, News, Beginners Please (piano & song), War on Two Fronts (talk on Catholicism by Jesuit, Fr Joseph Christie), Variety Concert (RE Light Orchestra), Question time (with Joe Linnane, and Song Time, with Al Thomas, at the Phoenix Hall)), Between Ourselves (weekly programme for women), Culwick Choral Society, Nuacht, News, Hospitals Trust Programme, Chick Smith and his Dance Orchestra, Late Sports Results at 11.30pm.

Friday: News at 8am, Morning Music, Batchelors Programme, Bradmola Programme, News, Signpost & Close Down at 9.30am. Chivers Programme at 1pm, Imco Programme, News & Topical talk, Imco Programme, Rowntrees Programme, Cotts of Kilcock Programme, close at 2.30pm. Aladdin (story & song with Fay Sargent & Kitty O'Callaghan) at 5.30pm, Interlude, Angelus, Amhrain Leis an gCruit, Announcements, News, Earth Air & Water (weekly talk by J. Ashton Freeman), Malartan na mBaruil, The Graves at Kilmorna

(Canon Sheehans novel in drama), The Winter Proms, Tour of Europe in Song – France (RE Singers, introduced by Sean Mac Reamoinn), Sports Stadium (presented by Philip Greene), Nuacht, News, Hospitals Trust Programme, An Club Taibhseoireachta, Light Music for Two Pianos (Mollie Phillips & Albert Healy), Late Sports Results, and Closedown at 11.30pm.

Saturday: News at 8am, The Standard Programme, Mackintoshes Programme, Keillers Programme, News, Signpost & Close Down at 9.30am. Urneys Programme at 1pm, Donnellys Programme, News & Weekend Sport, Birds Programme, Gateaux Programme, Waltons Programme, Close at 2.45pm. Reopen at 5.30 with Artane School Band & John Thompson (tenor), Interlude, Angelus, Irish Dance Music, Racing Results, News, Irish Ballads, "Who's News" (presented by Ronnie Walsh), Listen & Learn, In Reply to Yours (listener's letters), An Fear a Phos Balbhan (drama), The Balladmakers Saturday Night, Kathleen Green (viola), World Affairs (Robert Brennan), Nuacht, News, Hospitals Trust Programme, Tunes From Vienna (George Popps Septet), Fleagh na Nollag, Late Sports Results at 12midnight.

Sunday: High Mass at 10.30am (from Gort Muire, Dundrum, Co Dublin), 11.15 close down. Take the Floor at 1pm (Ceili House repeat), Question Time & Song Time at 2pm (repeat), Elijah at 3pm (with Our Ladys Choral Society – RE recording). Childrens Request Programme at 5.30pm (Williamstown Childrens Ceili Band), Interlude, Angelus, Rogha na Eisteoire, Appeal on behalf of NSPCC, News at 6.30pm, Soccer Survey, Provinchial News Round-Up, Organ Recital (Georges Minne), Broadcast Music of the Week (Seoirse Bodlai), Thomas Davis Lectures (Wealth from Seaweed by Thomas Dillon), St Marys Choir Clonmel, Parnell & English Politics, Ever the Twain (comedy by Lennox Robinson), Gaelic Sports News, News at 10.15pm, Hospitals Trust Programme, An Old Refrain (RE Light Orchestra), close down.

Later in the year, the Sunday programmes changed, as follows: Opens at 11.13am with High Mass from Glenstall Priory, Limerick. 12.30pm Concert of Irish music with Radio Eireann Light Orchestra. 1.00pm music with Garda Ceili Band and Military Bands. 1.35pm Ceolta Tire.

2.00pm The School Around the Corner with Paddy Crosbie (Belgrove NS Clontarf). 2.30 Leo Rowsome – Uileann Pipes. 2.45 Death Drives Fast, a thriller by Brian Balread. 3.30pm Question Time with Joe Linnane, and Song Time with Al Thomas. (Or on 530 m: Ulster Senior Football Championship from Casement Park, Belfast, Antrim v. Armagh, with commentary by Michael O hEithir.) 7.30, The Merchant of Venice (parts one and two). 10.30 Hospital Trusts Programme.

Some of the programmes on Radio Eireann on Christmas Eve 1954 included: 4.00pm Service of Nine Lessons from St Patricks Cathedral. 6.00pm Choir of Franciscan Friary, Merchants Quay. 7.00pm A Christmas Carol (Dickens) with Siobhan McKenna, Anew McMaster, Dominic Roche, Eve Watkinson, Milo O'Shea. 12.00 Midnight Mass from Holy Ghost Missionary College, Kimmage.

Some of the programmes on Radio Eireann for Christmas Day 1954 included: 10.30am High Mass from Holy Ghost College, Kimmage. 11.30am Church of Ireland Service from Harold's Cross, with sermon by Rev. C.G. Proctor. 12.15pm Messiah (Handel) with Our Ladys Choral Society. 1.45-3.15pm Hospitals Requests. 5.00 Junior Red Cross Party from Cappagh Hospital. 8.45-10.00pm The O'D Story: 27 years of comedy, songs and sketches, with Jimmy O'Dea, Harry O'Donovan, Maureen Potter, Fay Sargent, Danny Cummins, Denis Brennan, the RE Singers, RE Light Orchestra. 10.35 Ceili na Nollag, 11.15 recording of Stanley Black & his Orchestra.

Radio Luxembourg

Based in Luxembourg, this commercial station had a lot of music, but only broadcast in the evenings from 6pm to 12midnight, on 208 metres. Typical programmes in 1954 included:

Monday: Mondays Requests, Dan Dare Adventures, Smash Hits, Godfrey Winn (presents Your Mother's Birthday), From Hollywood, The Gift Box, The Case of the Sinister Sister, Forces Choice, Your Record

Shop, Music for Everyone, Music from the Ballet, Interlude, The Bible Christian programme, Frank & Ernest, World Tomorrow.

Tuesday: Tuesdays Requests, The Starline Show, Dan Dares Adventures, Songtime with Jo Stafford, Guess the Name, The Story of Dr Kildare, From Hollywood, Geraldo Orchestra, The Case of the Sinister Sister, Melodies by Mairants, Music for Everyone, Songs from the Screen, Revival Time, Oral Roberts.

Wednesday: Wednesdays Requests, Tollefesen (world's premier accordionist), Dan Dares Adventures, Family Album, Soccer Survey, People Are Funny, From Hollywood, The Gift Box, The Case of the Sinister Sister, The Alka-Seltzer Show, Dreamtime, Music of the Stars, Queens Hall Light Orchestra, The Answer Man, Back to the Bible, Music at Bedtime.

Thursday: Thursdays Requests, Musical Round Up, Adventures of Dan Dare (Pilot of the Future), Topical Half Hour, Movie Magazine, Norrie Takes a Chance (Norrie Paramour & His Orchestra), Case of the Sinister Sister, Melodies by Mairants (presented by David Jacobs), Tune in to Teddy, Music for Everyone, Old Fashioned Revival Hour.

Friday: Fridays Requests, Butlins Beaver Club, Adventures of Dan Dare, Topical Hour, David Rose Orchestra, Hopalong Cassidy, Evening Stars, Case of the Sinister Sister, Edmundo Ros Orchestra, Dreamtime, Forces Choice, Old Acquaintance, Lets Dance, The Voice of Prophecy, Radio Bible Class, The Answer Man.

Saturday: Saturdays Requests, Amateur Football Results, Irish Requests, Keytime, From Hollywood, Scottish Requests, 208 Radio Theatre, Popular Melodies, Bringing Christ to the Nations, 208 Supper Club (where you will meet many famous artistes).

Sunday: Welcome to 208, The Ovaltineys Concert Party, Primo Scala Band, Frankie Laine Sings, Your Favourites & Mine, Doris Day Sings, Winifred Atwell Show, Vera Lynn Sings, Take Your Pick (compered by Michael Miles), Carroll Gibbons & his Savoy Hotel Orchestra, Alka

Seltzer Show, Case of the Sinister Sister, Ted Heath Music, Listen with Philips, Bing Sings, The Answer Man, Top Twenty (at 11pm), Music at Midnight. (*Note: In October, the Top Twenty was on a Friday night at 11pm*). The Top Twenty were the pop songs from America and England, including new stars such as Little Richard, Chuck Berry, Fats Domino, Bo Diddley, and Elvis Presley.

American Forces Network (AFN)

This military-sponsored station was on shortwave, broadcasting from Europe, from 6pm to midnight. Following the Second World War, it was intended to entertain American soldiers and their families in European and worldwide bases, but was also enjoyed by civilians, and its programmes were listed in the Saturday edition of the Irish Times. Besides various news and sports bulletins, popular programmes were "Music in the Air", Grand Old Opry, Record Parade of Hits on Saturday evening, Jazz Nocturne, Rocker Club. And of course, lots of Elvis Presley, Church Berry, and the rising American pop stars.

British Broadcasting Corporation (BBC)

BBC Light was a favourite with many Irish listeners, as a supplement to Radio Eireann. Popular programmes were "The Archers" (a soap opera), "Hancock's Half Hour" (comedy sketches), and of course, "Listen with Mother". The latter 15-minute programme was aired at 1.45pm, and was aimed at nippers under the age of five, beginning with the words: "Now children, are you sitting comfortably, then I'll begin".

Pop Stars of 1954

Some of the big names in music in the 1950's included Kitty Kallen, Rosemary Clooney, Eddie Calvert, Dean Martin, Doris Day, Johnny

Mathis, Johnny Ray, Ruby Murray, Slim Whitman, Bing Crosby, Debbie Reynolds, Frankie Lane, Tony Bennett, Jim Reeves.

During 1954, the Irish Times listed popular songs, such as O Mein Papa by Eddie Calvert (released in 1953), Changing Partners (Donah Shore), Tennessee Wig Walk (Bonnie Lou), You Alone (Perry Como), Ricochet (Alma Cogan), Istanbul (Frankie Vaughan), Cottage by the Lee (Robert Wilson). During the week of 14/10/54, the Irish Times Record of the Week was Gilly Gilly by Max Bygraves. They listed the best sellers as Three Coins in the Fountain by Tony Brent, Little Things Mean a Lot by Alma Cogan, and Hole Gossip by Perry Como.

Other popular songs heard on the radio during 1954 were Mr Sandman by The Chordettes, Rose Marie by Slim Whitman, That's Amore by Dean Martin, This Ole House by Billie Anthony, The Naughty Lady of Shady Lane by The Ames Brothers, Mambo Italiano by Rosemary Clooney. In 1955, songs included Memories are Made of This by Dean Martin, The Yellow Rose of Texas by Gary Miller, and Sixteen Tons by Tennessee Ernie Ford. One of the most famous songs of 1956 was Banana Boat Song (Day-O) by Harry Belafonte.

Unlike today, when there are pop groups and rock bands, the 1950's was a time of small orchestras, which were integral to all the popular songs and hit records. Female singers were just as numerous as male performers, and children sometimes comprised the chorus.

Television

Ireland did not have any TV stations until Telefis Eireann (later called RTE) was set up in 31/12/1961.

Some people along the east coast of Ireland, especially in Dublin, had television aerials attached to their chimney stacks on the roof, pointing towards Britain, and therefore could pick up one or two English programmes (to the consternation of the Irish Catholic church), on their Black & White television sets (no colour yet). In May 1953 the BBC set up television transmitters in Belfast, and Irish households along the border with Northern Ireland could then receive the BBC.

Nowadays, aggressive and persistent advertising is the main income of commercial television stations, and even the National broadcaster (RTE) has to hold out the begging bowl. In the 1950's, advertising was concentrated on radio "sponsored programmes", widely-read newspapers, and many "Advertising Stations" (billboards) on the numerous derelict sites in the city centre and suburbs.

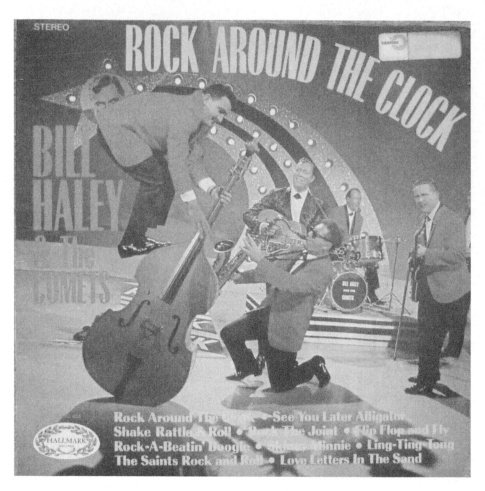

Bill Haley ushered in the "rock & roll" era in America in 1954, and LP records then became fashionable (now back in vogue as "vinyl").

Newspapers

In the Dublin of 1954, the public were avid readers of newspapers, and there were three daily newspapers (Irish Times, Irish Independent, Irish Press), three evening papers (Evening Press, Evening Herald, Evening Mail), and two Sunday papers (Sunday Press and the Sunday Independent).

The Irish Independent, Middle Abbey Street, which celebrated its Golden Jubilee on the 3rd January, 1955, had Fine Gael leanings, and had the biggest daily circulation at 190,000. It owned the Evening Herald and the Sunday Independent.

The Irish Times, 31 Westmoreland Street, had a Protestant ethos, with a small circulation amongst the business and academic communities.

The Irish Press, 13/14 Burgh Quay, was owned by the de Valera family (Fianna Fail), and was widely circulated in the rural and farming communities. They owned the very popular Sunday Press, and the equally popular Evening Press. The latter was launched on the 1st September, 1954, from Elephant House, corner of O'Connell Street and Middle Abbey Street (formerly Elverys), and quickly reached circulation figures of 103,377.

The Dublin Evening Mail, 38/40 Parliament Street, was the smallest paper, but closed in 1962.

British newspapers also circulated, including the Daily Express/Sunday Express, much to the dismay of the Catholic clergy!

Specialist publications included the "Irish Catholic" newspaper, "Dublin Opinion" (satirical magazine), "The Bell" magazine (a forum for literary talent, but closed in 1954), "Women" magazine (with 16-page detachable knitting booklet), "Readers Digest"(1/6d), "Our Boys" (magazine for boys, published by the Christian Brothers), "Jack & Jill" (childrens magazine launched in February 1954, at 5d a copy).

The evening newspapers were much more popular that the dailies, and street sellers (mostly very young lads) were positioned on most corners of the city centre, shouting out "erald or press", referring to the Evening Herald and Evening Press. Motor scooters, adapted with a wide rear basket to hold bundles of newspapers, rushed around the city at breakneck speed delivering the newspapers to the hundreds of small shops.

The following are some general examples of the contents of the various newspapers.

Irish Independent

The front page often consisted of full page advertisements, for example, for the Winter Sale in Clerys Department Store. Sometimes the Death Notices were on the front page.

Daily strip cartoons: "Rip Kirby" by Alex Redmond (about a racing driver), "Hopalong Cassidy" by Dan Spiegle, "Jet Scott" by The Ice Queen (about a ship), and "Curly Wee & Gussie Goose". Mickey Mouse appeared weekly.

"Lost & Found: Foxhound from Fingal Harriers Hunt Kennels. Gold Cross. Fishing rod on train from Kingsbridge."

"Conscience Money: Minister for Finance acknowledges 30/- posted to Registry of Deeds".

"Thanksgiving": people thanked different Saints for favours.

Crossword puzzles. Games of Bridge (Josephine Culbertson).

"Today's Weather". "Ships in Dublin Port", including their cargoes. "Tides".

The "Social & Personal" columns listed the comings and goings of important people, even listing the hotels where they were staying, such as the Gresham, Shelbourne, Royal Hibernian, Russell, and even the Portmarnock Country Club. Weekly column, "Wedding Bells" with photos of newly married couples.

Throughout the year there were articles such as Life Story of Pope Pius X, Edel Quinn and the Legion of Mary, Knitting, Alphabet of Herbs, How to make marmalade, French-polishing tips, Plant a hawthorn hedge, Bullock Harbour once Dublin's port, Crochet for a Marian Altar, The alphabet in Crocket, Pig breeding by Jim Norton, Cookery for Beginners: - Rough Puff Pastry for Tarts and Sausage Rolls, Russian Architecture over the centuries, News from Near and Far, Being of Sound Mind (about wills). The Book Page was on Saturdays, with book reviews of all the latest books.

"The Stars in October" , was a scientific article on astronomy at the end of each month, with a hemispherical black map showing the positions of the shining stars.

The full transcript of Archbishop McQuaid's Lenten Pastoral (sermon) was published in March.

During October 1954, Dorothy O'Farrell had a series of six articles, about her 15,000 mile round trip from London to Capetown in South Africa, including photos of places visited. One leg of the voyage saw her in Port Said in Egypt, where she visited a Mohammedan Mosque (Muslim), and noted many bicycles, expensive motor cars, and also horse-drawn carriages.

There was a series on the history of the Abbey Theatre, including their initial plays in St Teresa's Hall, Clarendon Street.

The comedian, John D. Sheridan, had a little article in October about a poem called "Birds in their Little Nests".

The Sunday Independent newspaper also had strip cartoons, such as "The Phantom" by Lee Falk/Wilson McCoy. The "Big Crossword" had a 1st prize of £600, and 2nd prize of £250.

Irish Press

The Irish Press had its own strip cartoons: "Little Panda", "The Cisco Kid", "Blondie", and there was a daily article in the Irish language, using the old Gaelic script. Do-it-yourself enthusiasts could get tips from a column entitled "Man About the House".

Various reviewers had their own columns, such as "Theatre Reviews" by Niall Carroll ("The Seven Year Itch" in the Gaiety, and

"Blithe Spirit" in the Olympia), "Music Reviews" by Robert Johnston (Ulster Girls Choir in the Metropolitan Hall in Lower Abbey Street), "Radio Reviews" by Julia Monks ("Living with Joe Lynch" on Radio Eireann).

Irish Times

On weekdays, the Irish Times had 10 pages, but 15-18 on Saturday. The Times Pictorial was also available on Saturdays, containing 24 pages of gossip, including gossip from America.

R. M. Smylie, editor of the Irish Times from 1934 to 1954, died in September. The funeral service took place in Ormond Quay & Scots Presbyterian Church in Lower Abbey Street, with a big attendance (but no Catholics), and then burial in Mount Jerome (mainly Protestant cemetery) in Harold's Cross.

Daily cartoons: "Oscar", "The Saint" (by Leslie Charteris), "Buck Rogers", "Rocket Ranger".

"Aris", a column in Irish by Risteard O'Glaisne, was printed on Saturdays, and sometimes on Tuesday.

Regular hunting (on horseback) photographs, for example, South County Dublin Harriers "meet" at Saggart, County Dublin, in November. Regular photos of big ships in and out of Dublin. Daily photos of wedding couples. Weekly "Portrait Gallery", an article about a living famous person (in January, Dr Bethel Solomons).

Regular column called "Cruiskeen Lawn", by Myles na Gopaleen, and another entitled "John D. Sheridan Says".

Every Tuesday or Wednesday, the Irish Times had "Sporting Log" by The Skipper, a gossip column with a brief round-up of various sports.

Sir Arthur Conan Doyle (author of detective books about Sherlock Holmes and his side-kick Dr Watson), had a weekly series on history, such as "Wild Geese" in September.

The Irish Times had two crosswords, one called Crossaire, (No 1243 on 14/10/1954), and also the Simplex Crossword (No 381 in January 1954.)

"Sean Bunny" cartoon with story by Marion King on Saturdays, e.g. on 4th October, "The Blue-Nosed Witch". "

"Books of the Week" every Saturday, and also film reviews.

Social & Personal Column. For example, 4th October, 1954: "Lieutenant-Colonel & Mrs G. E. Stevens have arrived in Dublin from England, and are staying in the Royal Hibernian Hotel. Colonel & Mrs Royston Pigott of Carnew County Wexford, are spending a few days in the Shelbourne Hotel".

"Engagements for Today" listed various shows and exhibitions, mostly in Dublin.

"Irishmans Diary" (sometimes "Irishwomans Diary"). Also "London Letter" from 59 Fleet Street.

On the 15th March 1954, the Irish Times published the full text of Archbishops McQuaids Lenten Pastoral (a Catholic sermon). The newspaper also had a series in March about the life of Pope Piux X, by Fr John Fennelly.

Every month there was a scientific article entitled, "The Sky in June" (or whatever month was appropriate), including an egg-shaped sketch of the sky and stars. The Irish Independent had monthly serious articles called, "The Stars in June" (as appropriate).

Evening Herald

This evening paper also had strip cartoons, including "Mutt & Jeff", "Roy Rogers" (by King of the Cowboys), "Pilot Storm", "Little Sport" by Rousm.

Information on various camping trips could be obtained in "Catholic Boy Scouts Notes". .

The classified small advertisements had headings such as "Employment Offered", "Employment Wanted", "Domestics Wanted", "Thanksgiving" (for religious favours). Post Office Box Numbers were provided for replies (instead of addresses).

Transport

Shipping

Merchant Shipping

In 1954, both Sir John Rogersons Quay and North Wall Quay were teeming with ships being loaded and unloaded by hundreds of workmen ("dockers"), aided by huge 4-legged cranes running along railway-style tracks. A few decades later, both men and cranes were gone, having been replaced by big steel containers, crammed with goods of evert sort, which were deposited on the backs of big lorries and driven away to warehouses in the suburbs. The following is a mere sample of the ships in 1954.

"17th de Octobre" arrived in Dublin from Buenos Aires (Argentina) with a cargo of bananas and pollard (fish), plus seventy five 1st Class passengers.

"The City of Chester" arrived in Dublin from Calcutta (India), with 46,000 chests of tea.

In February, "Bel Mare", chartered by Esso, arrived from Sweden into Alexandra Basin, Dublin, with 3.35million gallons of oil (14,000 ton).

In February, 900 tons of sisal (type of flax) arrived into Dublin, destined for Irish Ropes in Drogheda, to make ropes and twine.

In April, "Rathlin Head" (9,200 ton, built in Belfast) brought 6,000 tons of lumber (timber logs) from Canada to Dublin.

In June, the "Rasmus Tholstrup" tanker (Swedish ship) arrived in Dublin from Denmark with the first cargo of 320 metric tons of liquid gas called Kosangas in large cylindrical tanks, for a new company, McMullan Kosangas Ltd. The Danish company, Tholstrups, had a joint venture with the Irish company, McMullan, who owned the Maxol oil business.

During the year, the newspapers had a photo of a ship unloading tomatoes from the Canary Islands, long before package sun-holidays were invented.

Tedcastle McCormick was importing petroleum oil in big tanker ships, for storage in large circular tanks in the docks, and later distribution to petrol stations.

Shipbuilding

In 1954, the steel tug "Mersin 1", landed at Dalkey Shipyard Company at the West Pier in Dun Laoire. It was built for a Turkish client, and named after the port of Mersin in Turkey.

The "M.V. Lady Grania" was built for Guinness in 1952, and the M.V. Gwendolen in 1953, the first of the companies motor vessels to replace the steam ships. The company also had a fleet of barges, to ferry barrels of beer down the River Liffey from St James's Gate Brewery to the docks, including "Castleknock" and "Killiney". These barges had a hinged funnel to allow the latter to be lowered while passing under O'Connell Bridge at high tide.

In June, the new Irish lightship, "Gannet", was permanently moored on Kish Bank.

Irish Shipping Ltd launched "Irish Holly" at West Hartlepool in January (oil fired steam engines), and after other works were completed, the ship arrived in Dublin on the 20th May. This ship was chartered by Irish Shell as Ireland's first oil tanker.

The 218 feet long 1,000 ton collier ship (for transporting coal), "M.V. Irish Fern", built in the Liffey Dockyard (Alexandra Basin on the North Wall) for Irish Shipping Ltd, was launched in August, and then made its maiden voyage to Cardiff in December.

Coastal Shipping Company received a new cargo ship in April, the "Killiney Coast", 200 feet long, built in Lubeck, Germany. She had a sister ship, "Dalkey Coast".

The Irish Lights tender "Ierne" was sent to be scrapped at the Hammond Lane Metal Company on Sir John Rogersons Quay.

John Tyrrell & Sons, Arklow, County Wicklow, built "Marian" in March.

Courtesy Visits

Near the end of July, part of the US Navy paid a six-day courtesy visit to Dublin, comprising seven Destroyers headed by the 17,000 ton "Worcester". They were welcomed into Dublin Bay by a gun salute fired from the Irish Army Battery at the end of the East Pier in Dun Laoghaire. The Worcester was then visited by TDs, church leaders, and many notable public figures. The Jewish sailors on board attended a service at the Jewish Progressive Congregation in Leicester Avenue, Rathgar (behind the Church of the Three Patrons), and then a reception given by Dr Bethel Solomons. 400 sailors each donated a pint of blood in Alexandra Basin to the National Blood Transfusion Service.

In August, the "KNM Stord" (D300), a destroyer of the Royal Norwegian Navy, visited Dublin.

The Spanish square-rigged training barque "Galatea" arrived in Dublin in September.

Miscellaneous

At the end of November, the "Tresillian" British cargo ship foundered during gales about 81 kilometres off the Cork coast, with 24 dead and 16 survivors. 12 of the survivors were transferred to Cobh by Irish Naval Ship, LE Maeve (LE Maev).

The 20,000 ton luxury liner, "Empress of Canada", caught fire in Liverpool in January 1953. In September, while being towed to Genoa in Italy to be scrapped, it was forced to seek refuge in Dun Laoire during a storm, after the burnt-out hulk broke adrift in Dublin Bay.

Flying

Collinstown Airport opened in January 1940 (during the Second World War), and after the war, had only a few flights to Liverpool using a small airplane. Shannon Airport had opened the previous year, and in due course, was used for flights to and from America. Even in 1954, Dublin Airport was sometimes referred to as Collinstown Airport. The curved terminal building had open balconies facing the runway for public viewing, and viewing was also allowed from the flat roof. Aer Lingus was 60% owned by Aer Rianta, and 40% owned by British European Airways (BEA).

In March, 1954, Aer Lingus launched two new Vickers Viscounts jets, St Patrick and St Brigid, each being 48 seaters. St Brendan, and St Lawrence O'Toole, would follow later.

In 1954, Aer Lingus operated the last flight to Northolt, England, after seven years, because that airport was being returned to military use.

Flying in 1954 was the preserve of business people and wealthy tourists, because of the expense involved. Even so, in 1953, Aer Lingus was operating Winter flights to London for £10 return, with 6-8 flights daily, and flight time of 80 minutes. The following year, Aer Lingus provided Tourist Returns to London, for £11.15, or tourist returns by British European Airways (BEA) to Europe (e.g. Dublin to Rome £54.15, Barcelona £46, Nice £44, Brussels £24/5). The Aer Lingus booking office was at 40 Upper O'Connell Street, Dublin, and also in Cruises Hotel, Limerick. Pan American (35 Westmoreland Street) operated flights from Shannon to Chicago, Detroit, and New York.

In 1954, Aer Lingus handled air-freight, and even horses were transported to England for races, using a Bristol Wayfarer.

Even in 1954, the annual blessing by a priest of the small Aer Lingus fleet was an important public event, because flying was still regarded as risky, and God's blessing was desirable. Some airplane crashes were as follows:

On New Years Day 1953, an Aer Lingus DC3, St Kieran, crash landed in a field near Birmingham. There were no passenger deaths or injury, but two members of the crew were slightly injured.

A few days later, a BEA Viking crashed near Nutts Corner, Belfast, killing 27 of the 35 people on board.

In January, 1954, a BOAC Comet jet crashed into the Mediterranean Sea off the Italian island of Elba, and killed all 35 on board (29 passengers and 6 crew). "Metal fatigue" was later identified as the cause of the crash.

In February 1954, the Bristol Britannia crash landed in mud in the Severn Estuary, while being tested, but there were no deaths or injuries.

In April 1954, another Comet plane crashed near Naples, killing all the 14 passengers and 7 crew.

On 5th September, a KLM Constellation Triton airplane, enroute Amsterdam to New York, with a stopover at Shannon, crashed into the Shannon Estuary, with the loss of 28 lives (some actually drowned), and 28 survivors (46 passengers and 10 crew in total on plane). A public enquiry was started in November in Kings Inns, Dublin, lasting many months, with a finding that the crash was caused by the landing gear unexpectedly re-opening after take-off, and then the pilot failing to react quickly enough.

In September, an Aer Lingus DC3, St Enda, crash landed in a field at the end of the grass runway in Guernsey (Channel Islands). It was flying from Dublin to the sister island of Jersey, but was diverted by fog to Guernsey. There was a good landing and no one was injured. The crew consisted of captain, 1st officer, and one hostess.

In 1954, the Minister for Health warned of the risk of smallpox, because every day people arrived by air from all parts of the world where smallpox was endemic, and he therefore advised on the immunisation (vaccination) of children.

Trains

Coras Iompair Eireann (CIE) used Kingsbridge Station (renamed Heuston in 1941) for journeys to the west of Ireland, while the Great Northern Railway (GNR) used Amiens Street Station (now called Connolly) for journeys up to Belfast. Westland Row (now called Pearse) was used for the Dun-Laoire boat (emigrant ship to Holyhead in England), and also journeys down the east coast. Harcourt Street Station (closed since 1958, and nowadays used as a restaurant) was used for trips down to Wicklow, and part of that line is now used by the LUAS tram. Broadstone had closed in 1937, having been used by the Midland Great Western Railway.

In 1953/1954, CIE trains changed from coal-fired steam engines to oil-fired locomotives (which were faster), and 94 diesel locos were ordered from Metropolitan-Vickers Electrical Co Ltd in England. CIE used its vast Inchicore Works for building train coaches and goods wagons, and servicing engines.

In 1954, when very few people owned a car, trains were used for leisure, such as a day-trip to some exotic location elsewhere in Ireland. Before "The Troubles" started in Northern Ireland in 1969, people often made a day-trip to Belfast. For example, the train departed Dublin at 9.00am, left Belfast that evening at 6.00pm, arriving back in Dublin at 9.20pm, all for 15/- return (3rd class) or 22/6 (1st class), and children under 14 years for half price. Trains never had 2nd class carriages!

The "Mystery Train" was re-introduced in 1948 after "The Emergency" (Second World War), and passengers only knew their destination when they actually arrived there. The train left Dublin (and other cities) at 2.15pm, and arrived back at 9.45pm, allowing four or five hours to enjoy the secret destination.

The "Radio Train" was a more luxurious day-trip during the Summer from Dublin to Sligo, Galway and Killarney. The cost included train fare, lunch and High Tea onboard, musical programme, commentary on places of interest, and tours in the three cities (jaunting car in Killarney): 54/- to Killarney (children under 14, 35/-), 50/- to Sligo, and 46/- to Galway. There was a special studio at the rear of the train, and loudspeakers in each carriage.

Trains ran from Amiens Street to catch the ship (having originated in Liverpool or Southampton in England) in Cobh for those emigrating to America and Canada. Emigration officials checked passenger passports and papers at Amiens Street. Nowadays trains travel from Heuston Station to Cork, and then change for Cobh.

There was a lot of bad flooding in December 1954 throughout Ireland, and especially in the River Shannon catchment area, the worst since 1880 (sounds familiar even in 2021!). There was similar flooding in the Fairview area of Dublin, when the River Tolka burst its banks after 36 hours of heavy rain, and boats were used to rescue householders. The mainline railway bridge across the East Wall Road collapsed, and the Army had to blow up the remainder of the huge steel beams to allow flood water collecting on the road to escape.

Buses

Dublin had a great tram system, running from the city centre to the various outlying suburbs, but the Government closed in down in the 1940's, and the last tram ran in 1949. However, the public bus service had started in the 1920's, and gradually built up a great network of routes, which the trams could not compete with.

In the 1950's, the green-coloured double-decker buses were very user-friendly, with both a driver and a jovial bus conductor, the latter collecting the cheap fares and ringing the bell for stop and start. The open rear platform, with vertical chromium bar to swing off, was an added attraction for the athletic type, if you just missed your bus or wanted to get off a few seconds before the bus stopped. Cigarette and pipe smoking was permitted upstairs only.

Most city buses terminated at Nelsons Pillar in the centre of O'Connell Street. Buses to long-distance rural destinations terminated at Busarus in nearby Store Street/Amiens Street. Busarus was the first modern office block in Dublin, when it opened in October 1953, at a cost of £1million. The passenger hall was on the ground floor, with Arus Mhic Dhiarmada (offices) on the upper floors, including a fancy Civil Service restaurant on the top floor. The 280 seater newsreel cinema in the basement was completed in March 1954, but it did not open until September 1959 as the Eblana Theatre, showing Synge's "Deirdre". CIE also used Busarus as its terminus for tourist coach tours.

Cars

Dublin had plenty of cars in 1954, but the owners were mostly "well-to-do" individuals and families. Parking was free, and cars parked along both sides of most streets, including Grafton Street, although

O'Connell Street availed of the wide central reservation. Grafton Street was a "one-way" street, from south to north.

There were no traffic lights at street junctions. Instead, there was a Garda on "point-duty" at busy city-centre locations, and he wore a white armband from elbow to wrist, and twirled a white baton. There were plenty of "Zebra crossings" for pedestrians, and the ones at O'Connell Bridge included low bollards with the words "Treasna Annso", old Irish for "Cross Here". Nowadays spelt "anseo".

Road markings, such as central white lines, and double-yellow side lines (no parking) were a thing of the future.

There was no driving test for car owners up to 1964, and seat-belts had yet to be invented.

Petrol rationing after "The Emergency" was still in operation up to 1957. Petrol was dispensed from pumps at the outer edge of the footpath, with Esso and Caltex (later called Texaco) being popular brands. For example, there were Esso petrol pumps at the edge of the footpath at Robert Callow, Motor engineers, 44 Westland Row.

Dunlop tyres were popular, and the company had its offices at Dunlop House on Lower Abbey Street (now the site of the VHI offices).

Since very few people had a house phone, public phone boxes were part of the street landscape. For example, there was a row of 8 phone boxes outside the former Ballast Office on Aston Quay. Nearby was the O'Connell Bridge School of Motoring at 1 Aston Quay (corner of Bedford Row), boasting of dual-control cars.

The Automobile Association had its offices in 23 Suffolk Street, and boasted of a dozed dedicated telephone kiosks around the country, and a new one opened in August 1954 at Rathcoole on the Naas Road (no dual-carriageway back then). They had recently added Land Rovers to their fleet, for towing distressed cars.

However, there is no stopping progress, even in 1954, and local residents held a meeting in St Laurence Hall, Stillorgan, protesting about the proposed Stillorgan dual-carriageway (which eventually opened in the 1980's). In January, 1954, Donnybrook Bus Garage provided free car parking on a trial basis, with one area for 50 cars and another for 60 cars, in order to ease the traffic problems in the city centre.

In 1954, the motor car was still in its infancy, and there were still traces of previous methods of transport, especially in the commercial world, such as horse stables in the lanes at the rear of big shops and factories. Some horse-drawn milk floats still delivered bottles of milk to domestic customers, and of course, "rag and bone merchants" still trundled around the city with horse & cart, collecting scrap metal etc, and even small dealers were still delivering bags of coal by this relaxing mode of transport.

Car Assembly

Ireland never manufactured motor cars, but instead imported completed "kits" from European manufacturers, and assembled the cars here. This was the Governments way of creating jobs in Ireland.

Ford cars were assembled in Cork city, beside Dunlop tyres: Popular (£350), Anglia (£460), Prefect (£495), Consul (£585), Zephyr (£666), and Zodiac (£750). The list of Ford dealers in Dublin included Walden at 172/174 Parnell Street, Archer, 72-74 Fenian Street, Smithfield Motors (later called Linders), Esmonde Motors in Serpentine Avenue, Ballsbridge.

Lincoln & Nolan of 55-57 Lower Baggot Street (now Dept of Health office block), and assembly works at New Wapping Street (North Wall). They assembled the prestigious Rover 60 car, which was 4-cylinder, 2-litre, selling at £1,050, and Road Tax of £30. They sold the Austin A30 for £429 for two-door, and £449 for four-door, with speeds of up to 60 mph (miles per hour). The Austin A40 van cost £560. In 1954, Lincoln & Nolan presented an Austin engine to Bolton Street Technical College (VEC) for the training of mechanics.

G.A. Brittain Ltd, Grove Road, Portobello Bridge, Rathmines. Their very popular Morris Minor 2-door cost £439-10s, and £470 for the 4-door, with a top speed of 64mph, and fuel consumption of 45 miles per gallon (5 litres). One car every 20 minutes rolled off the assembly line. The new Morris Oxford was priced at £640.

The famous Volkswagen Beetle (Hitlers brainchild for the masses) was assembled by Motor Distributors Ltd, Shelbourne Road, Ballsbridge, retailing at £449, with a heater as standard. Their advertising agent was the well-known firm of O'Kennedy-Brindley. The newspapers in 1954 included a photo of the Volkswagen chief from Germany visiting the Dublin assembly plant, with Irish businessman, Stephen O'Flaherty.

The new Fiat 1100 was priced at £575, and was assembled by W.J. Henderson Ltd at Castleforbes Road (North Wall to Sheriff Street), and distributed by F.M Summerfield Ltd., 138 Lr Baggot Street (both part of McGee Group). The car was manufactured in Turin (northern Italy), and shipped to Ireland in crates for re-assembly.

Booth Bros, 63-67 Upper Stephen Street plus 15-17 South King Street, assembled MG and Wolseley cars, with the MG Magnette selling for £865, and the Wolseley 4/44 selling for £797. They also handled Nuffield tractors. Their assembly works was at 535 North Circular Road.

W.F. Poole & Co. assembled Denis and Morris commercial vehicles at 60-67 Lansdowne Park (off Haddington Road), and had showrooms at 42-43 Westland Row, and a service department in Greenmount Lane, Harold's Cross.

In 1954, the two companies amalgamated as Booth Poole, with a new headquarters in Islandbridge (later occupied by Glorneys Builders Providers, and now blocks of apartments).

McCairns Motors in Santry, 17-29 Tara Street, and Alexandra Road (north docks), assembled Vauxhall cars, included the Cresta 2¼ litre. They also handled Bedford, Chevrolet, and Buick.

McEntagart Bros, Percy Place, dealt in Standard, Triumph, and Packard cars, with their assembly plant beside 279 Cashel Road, Kimmage (beside Leo Labs). Their "New Standard Eight" sold for £438.

The Hillman Husky retailed at £465, with fuel consumption of 40 miles per gallon, and was distributed by Buckleys Motors Ltd.

Reg Arnstrong, 9-19 Ringsend Road, started out in 1953 with the assembly of NSU motorcycles, and then assembled the NSU Prinz car from 1958.

Ferguson tractors arrived by ship from London, fully assembled, and stored in a new (1954) warehouse in Lower Baggot Street (Lad Lane).

Car hire

William Fanagan of Aungier Street were described as Funeral Furnishers. They also operated a Self-Drive Car Hire business, using Hillman cars. In March, 1954, Ever Ready Cars in Donnybrook delivered to William Fanagan, three new Humber Pullman Limousines, registration ZU6711, ZU6712, ZU6713, very plush and majestic.

Murrays at Baggot Street Bridge described themselves as Funeral Undertakers, and also operated a Car Hire business.

Kirwins Funeral Directors in Fairview operated a fleet of Chrysler Windsor Hearses and Limousines.

Bicycles & Motorbikes

Dubliners of all ages in 1954 exercised much more than their modern counterparts, many walking to work, walking to their local grocery shops, or cycling to these destinations.

Bicycles were assembled from imported "kits", by such well-known names as Raleigh (8-11 Hanover Quay), Rudge Whitworth (62 North Wall Quay), Hercules and Norman (both by Irish Cycle Corporation, 123 Capel Street, and Santry Avenue).

Motorcycles were popular with young people, although most machines were small and not too fast, which was probably a good thing, since no one was legally obliged to wear a helmet.

In 1954, Reg Armstrong started assembly of the very popular German made "NSU" moped in Liberty Lane, and had showrooms at 63 Drury Street. The 50cc NSU Quickly cost £55 and provided over 200mpg. The 98cc was £108, the 125cc was £105, the 200cc was £145, and the 250cc was £185.

Lambretta scooters cost £135, and were assembled by Buckleys Motors Ltd, Shanowen Road, Santry.

The Italian-made Douglas Vespa moped, retailed at £129, cruised at 36mph, and did over 100 miles to the gallon with a pillion passenger. It was assembled and distributed by Erne Motor & Cycle Company, 17 Lower Baggot Street. There was a spare wheel attached to the rear.

The Austrian-made "PUCH" cost €129, and was available from Huet Motors. Huet also handled the 125 cc BSA Bantam, made by the British Small Arms Company (although originally a German design).

The Italian Moto Guzzi was also available in Ireland, with the Galleto 175cc selling for £150, and the Zigolo 98cc selling for £100.

For some unknown reason, some cycle and motorcycle dealers also dealt in the assembly and sale of radios.

Dublin Airport in the 1950's was a fashionable destination in itself, for dinner-dances, romantic nights in the restaurant, and people-watching.

The balconies and flat roof of Dublin Airport were used as viewing areas for the public, before being restricted in the 1970's for security reasons.

Guinness barges, "Castleknock" and "Killiney", and also "The Lady Grania" ship, on Custom House Quay in the 1950's. (Courtesy of Diagio/Guinness).

O'Donovan Rossa bridge, looking up Winetavern Street to Christchurch, with the Irish House pub on the left corner. (Courtesy of Dublin City Library & Archives).

O'Connell Street in 1954 was a hive of activity.

The Liffey ferry linked the docklands. (Courtesy of Dublin City Library & Archives).

Education

Trinity College

There were 7,601 students attending all universities in Ireland in 1954, and only 26% were female.

In 1954, Trinity College (officially called the "University of Dublin") in College Green was still a bastion of the old Protestant establishment. Catholic students were a rarity, ever since Archbishop John Charles McQuaid issued an edict forbidding Catholics to attend, on pain of a "mortal sin" and being ex-communicated from his church (his ban was eventually lifted in 1970).

Despite being founded in 1592, women were only admitted in 1904, but were not permitted to eat in the Dining Hall until 1954.

The Moyne Institute of Preventative Medicine opened in June 1953, at the south-east corner of College Park, beside the cricket pavilion.

There were plans in 1954 for a £450,000 new library, which eventually opened as the ultra-modern "brutalist" (brutal in some people's eyes) Berkeley Library in 1967.

In October, 1954, Oswald Mosley, the former British Fascist leader, spoke at the Philosophical Society in Trinity, which must have caused quite a stir at the time.

University College Dublin (UCD)

The "Catholic University" was founded on the south side of St Stephens Green by Cardinal Newman in 1854, and there were centenary celebrations in July 1954. Within a few decades they also has premises in Earlsfort Terrace, and in 1914 a new campus was built in this location (now the National Concert Hall). Their College of

Science was in Upper Merrion street, but is nowadays the Taoiseach's offices.

Newman House was still part of UCD in 1954, and in June there was a fire in the Aula Maxima Exam Hall (40 ft by 30 ft) of Newman House, when the mansard roof, with flat coffered plaster ceiling, was destroyed, and was later rebuilt. Since 2019, the building is the Museum of Literature, jointly used by UCD and the National Library.

Other Third-Level Educational Institutions

The site and old buildings of the Albert Agricultural College and its Model Farm in Glasnevin is nowadays part of the campus of Dublin City University (DCU).

In June, 1954, a new Pharmacy College opened in a fine old house at the plush address of 18 Shrewsbury Road in Ballsbridge.

The College of Art was situated right behind the National Library, adjoining the Dail, but nowadays it is located in the former Power's Whiskey Distillery in Thomas Street.

St Mary's College of Domestic Science, 8/9 Cathal Brugha Street, was later renamed the College of Catering. During 1954, there was a photo in the newspapers of the Floral Decoration Class in the Household Management Course.

Kevin Street and Bolton Street were Technical Colleges preparing students for a practical future in construction and engineering, both still going strong.

The newspapers contained a photo of an army group attending a course in the Civil Defence School, Phoenix Park.

Primary & Secondary Education

Most Irish people in the 1950's only received a Primary education, sometimes repeating a year or two, and leaving at the age of thirteen or fourteen. Some of the Primary schools had a "Secondary Top", whereby some pupils stayed in the same building, and studied for the

Intermediate Certificate (Junior Cert). Only the more prosperous families could afford the fees for Secondary schools, until the State introduced free Secondary education in 1967.

Generally, the Protestant schools were located in the Harcourt Street area, such as High School at 40 Harcourt Street (now partly the site of Divisional Garda HQ), Alexandra College in Earlsfort Terrace (now the site of the Conrad Hotel and office blocks), Diocesan Girls School, at the corner of Earlsfort Terrace and Adelaide Road (now a modern office block), Wesley College at St Stephens Green South, beside Methodist Centenary Church (now Stokes Place office blocks).

On the 1st December, 1954, distribution of prizes took place at the Masonic Boys School, Richview, Clonskeagh (now UCD School of Architecture).

The Kings Hospital School (Blue Coat School), a Protestant establishment, was in Blackhall Place, and then became the headquarters of the Law Society (solicitors) in 1978.

There were plenty of Catholic convent schools around the city centre, such as the Sacred Heart Convent at 15-19 Leeson Street Lower, (now part of Mount Anville in Goatstown), Loreto College, 53/54 St Stephens Green (still here). Belvedere College, near Parnell Square, catered for boys (still here).

The Marist Brothers (devotees of Mary) opened the Marian College in September 1954 in Lansdowne Road, Ballsbridge, initially using the existing Riverside House, and then building a two-storey school in 1956.

Specialist Institutions

Various Civil Service and Secretarial Colleges prepared girls for office work, such as Rosse (65 St Stephens Green), and Skerrys (76 St Stephens Green).

Kilroys Irish Correspondence College, 40-44 Molesworth Street, provided remote learning through the post, catering for second and third level subjects. They were based in a charming brick building, 2-floors plus dormer storey, with five pairs of windows at first floor level. No 39-40 was the attractive Molesworth Hall, including the

Church of Ireland Temperance Society. No 45 was another distinctive building in this stretch of the street from Molesworth Place to Dawson Street, which was swept away in the 1970's for an office block (which required upgrading in 2018!).

Miscellaneous

Besides the widespread use of pencils, students used a wooden pen with steel nib attached, which was dipped into a pot or bottle of dark blue ink. Blotting paper was needed to help dry out the page of writing. Some fancy Biros were being sold for 7/6, and looked like fountain pens.

School-children were given the "Fainne", a tiny round gold ring, attached to your coat lapel, as proof of proficiency in speaking the Irish language. In a December newspaper, there was a group photograph of Synge Street CBS boys after receiving their Fainne. Rarely was the Fainne worn by adults, except by a few fans working in the Civil Service.

Dublin had plenty of public libraries in the city centre, such as 106 Capel Street, 23 Thomas Street, 138-142 Pearse Street (Central), and 18 Kevin Street Lower. Only the latter two survive today.

The attractive Kevin Street library recently re-opened, while the modern "tech" to the right is now being demolished.

The former Thomas Street public library is still standing.

Employment

In 1954, Dublin was a small and compact city, with a vibrant mix of building uses. Most buildings in the city centre were fully utilised, with a variety of offices, small businesses and flats on all the upper floors above the shops. Almost everything was contained within the Grand Canal and the Royal Canal, including multi-storey factories and warehouses. Every necessity was easily accessible by walking, cycling, and the public bus, including schools, churches, entertainment, employment, etc. Dubliners were more industrious, hard-working, and more self-sufficient than today, where we rely far too much on cheap imports of practically everything. We even import domestic vegetables, despite the fact that our fields are lush and nutritious!

This wonderful conglomeration of successful city life was swept away within the following two decades in the name of "progress" and greed, whilst also allowing the city to sprawl out in all directions. Nowadays, Dublin City Council is wasting its energies in trying to "turn back the clock" and un-do the damage their predecessors in Dublin Corporation caused, or allowed to happen under their noses, since the cancer cannot be halted at this late stage.

Dublin Corporation

Dublin Corporation was a big employer, being well-funded from the commercial and domestic "rates" (tax on all property). "The Corpo" outdoor staff were visible all over the city, repairing and painting their vast stock of "social housing" (before a large part of it was stupidly sold off cheaply), collecting refuse in their "bin lorries" (before they made ratepayers pay again through private contractors), sweeping the roads and pavements, (even in such inner suburbs as Harold's Cross), repairing roads, lights, and sewers (even cleaning out the Autumn leaves from clogged road gullies every year!), and a multitude of other useful tasks.

Small road and sewer repairs around town were seldom completed in one day, and each excavation was guarded at night by an elderly watchman sitting in a little canvas hut, keeping himself (and the passing drunks and tramps) warm with glowing coke in a steel "brazier", with red coloured oil lambs to warn motorists, plus bulky red & white striped former oil drums around the hole in the road.

The various Dublin Corporation departments and maintenance depots were scattered around the city centre, before the appalling Civic Offices were built on the historic Wood Quay Viking site. A miniature scale-model of the proposed new offices was displayed to the public in 1955, but that proposal was far nicer that what was eventually built in the 1970's. An archaeological dig by the National Museum started in the early 1960's, and was still causing great public outrage in the 1970's when construction work finally started on "The Bunkers", which now look very dated.

The legendary "Corpo" outdoor worker has now disappeared (a man resting his elbow on a shovel), having been replaced by sub-contractors, and even their army of office workers move around the city incognito in their casual clothing.

Civil Service

Dublin was the epicentre for the thousands of office clerks who comprised the vast Civil Service which ran the country, despite the best efforts of the many part-time politicians who strove to "put a spanner in the works". Dubliners were more inclined to be engaged in productive work, and shunned the Civil Service, leaving those jobs for "country people" from rural Ireland.

Such was the power of the Catholic Church, that the "Marriage Bar" from 1932 to 1973, prohibited Civil Service women from working after they married, and every year many were obliged to resign from the Civil Service. After 1957, female National School teachers were excluded from the legislation. However, it must be remembered that most families in 1954 comprised a large number of children, and a mothers love and skills in the home were more important that soul-destroying office work in the bloated Civil Service.

Banking

Banking was the "Rolls-Royce" of permanent and pensionable employment, attracting brighter and more ambitious applicants compared with the Civil Service and Dublin Corporation. Cheques were rarely used, since people paid cash for their gas, electricity, coal, rates, etc, and obviously for groceries and clothing. Therefore, banking was more cash-oriented, and lending was aimed more at the farmers and business community.

There were more banking companies in 1954, each with branches around the city. Bank of Ireland was headquartered in College Green, Royal Bank of Ireland in Foster Place, Provinchial Bank of Ireland in London, Northern Bank in Belfast, Ulster Bank in Belfast, Hibernian Bank in 27 College Green, Munster & Leinster Bank in Cork, and National Bank in London. In 1966, the Royal, Provinchial, and Munster & Leinster, merged into Allied Irish Bank (AIB). In 1969, the Hibernian Bank and National Bank merged with Bank of Ireland.

During the year, there was a serious dispute in the banking industry, which resulted in a bank strike in January 1955.

The Central Bank of Ireland dates only from 1943, and was based in Foster Place, in the 1810 Guard House/Armoury wing of the Bank of Ireland headquarters (which itself was the original Irish Parliament prior to the Act of Union in 1800), and linked to a 1941 purpose-built office block immediately behind it in 18-21 Anglesea Street, nearly beside the Stock Exchange. An appalling hi-rise Central Bank was built in Dame Street in 1978, amid much controversary, including protests at the demolition of Commercial Buildings (built in 1799). The original Central Bank in Foster Place is now the Stock Exchange (following a short spell as a Wax Museum). The currency centre for minting notes and coins has been in Sandyford since the mid 1970's, and before that, De La Rue printers in Clonskeagh had a contract for this highly specialised work. The Central Bank moved to ugly new premises on North Wall Quay in 2017, ironically the abandoned skeleton of an office block being built for the infamous Anglo Irish Bank, the very company which contributed substantially to the economic "crash" of 2008, under the "light-touch" nose of the Central Bank banking Regulator! The new façade has the appearance of a building site still enveloped in scaffolding and dirty dust sheets!

There was no shortage of insurance companies in 1954, such as New Ireland Assurance, 12 Dawson Street, Irish Assurance Company in Upper O'Connell Street, and a multitude of other companies, all providing good office jobs.

Dublin had a few Building Societies, which only dealt in mortgages for house purchase. The Irish Industrial Building Society was based at 8 Camden Street Upper, and later changed its name to Irish Nationwide, which collapsed at the end of the "Celtic Tiger" in 2008, because of its reckless lending policies, and engaging directly in speculative property developments. The Irish Permanent Building Society was based at 12/13 Lower O'Connell Street, and is now called Permanent TSB, with modern headquarters in St Stephens Green on the site of the former St Vincents Hospital, and also providing banking services these days.

Office Workers

With the exception of the newly-built Bus Arus, Dublin had no modern office blocks, and the large number of office workers, including Civil Servants, were housed in Dublin's original stock of buildings, including the upper floors of shops in O'Connell Street. The Georgian buildings of St Stephens Green, Merrion Square, Parnell Square, Mountjoy Square, were full to capacity with offices of all sizes, and also residential flats on many top floors. Solicitors, accountants, doctors, and dentists, tended to congregate around the finer squares on the south side of the city, especially Fitzwilliam Square. The American Embassy was in 15 Merrion Square, and the British Embassy in 39 Merrion Square.

Office work was labour intensive in 1954, especially in the rigid and old-fashioned Civil Service, with much work done by pen and ink, and even pencils. However, there were typewriters in use in more progressive businesses, and Gestetner duplicating machines made copying easier in some companies.

28 D'Olier Street was called Carlisle Building, a substantial building which was occupied by the Commissioners of Irish Lights, who managed the lighthouses around the Irish coast. The Hospitals Trust (1940) Ltd., who ran the Irish Sweepstakes, had their Receiving Office (cash office) here. Nowadays the site is occupied by O'Connell Bridge House, one of the capitals first office blocks built in 1965.

Dockers

Dublin docklands bustled with many activities, such as manual loading and unloading of goods exported and imported by ship (including live animals such as cattle and sheep), temporary warehousing of such goods, unloading and storage of vast quantities of coal from England and Poland, importation and storage of oil, production of town-gas from coal, and a variety of businesses which were either regarded as "dirty" or needed plenty of open space. The north and south quays had huge four-legged cranes which moved along a railway track. Sometimes the goods were packed in bales or chests, and the cranes helped to lift these out of the ships hold. Other bulk goods, especially coal, had to be manually shovelled from the hold into large steel skips and then lifted out by crane. Hence, the docks were teaming with casual workers called "dockers", many getting only a days work at a time, depending on which ships were arriving and departing. There was a dockers dispute in November, perhaps reflecting the bigger dispute amongst dockers in England.

Coal was big business in Dublin, before the domestic central-heating era, and while the coal was stored in vast heaps beside the quays, smart offices in the city centre attracted cash customers, generally around D'Olier Street and Westmoreland Street, such as Wallace, Tedcastle McCormick, Sheridan Bros, Doherty, MacKenzie, Nicholl, Heiton, and Donnelly. Needless to say, chimney sweeps roamed around Dublin, making sure that Santa Claus could emerge spotless in the fireplace!

The ESB imported huge quantities of coal to fire their Pigeon House electricity generating station at the mouth of the River Liffey, which was superseded in the early 1970's by the Poolbeg Generating Station and its iconic red & white free-standing tall chimneys on the same site.

The Alliance & Dublin Consumers Gas Company, known simply to Dubliners as the Gas Company, manufactured town gas from coal at their big site stretching from Sir John Rogersons Quay to Pearse Street, storing the product in huge "Gasometers", before being piped underground to the thousands of homes in the suburbs. The company showrooms, offices and cash office was in an "art-deco" building at 24a D'Olier Street. The company had its own ships (colliers) importing coal directly into the adjoining Grand Canal Harbour.

Alexandra Road on the North Docks was home to the oil companies, such as Irish Shell, Esso, Caltex (later called Texaco), in addition to companies such as Gouldings Manure Works (fertilisers), Hammond Lane Metal Company (storage only, with production works at 111 Pearse Street), Prescotts (cleaners & dyers), Procea (starch, adhesives etc). There was also space for McCairns Motor Assembly (Vauxhall, Bedford, Chevrolet, Buick).

Brewing & Distilling

In 1954, Guinness was a great Protestant employer in James Street, with almost 4,000 employees, and the company also provided cheap rented accommodation scattered throughout The Liberties and elsewhere for its workers. In 1949/1950, the company built 238 houses for rent to their own workers in Kimmage (Corrib Road, Derravaragh Road, and Melvin Road), which were sold cheaply to the occupiers in 1970.

The timber casks (barrels) were made by skilled coopers. The casks of beer were transported down the River Liffey by barges (with hinged funnels to allow passage under low bridges at high tide) to their own fleet of ships alongside the quays in the docks, for export to England and the rest of the world. A feature of this part of Dublin was (and still is) the pleasant, maybe intoxicating, aroma from the brewing process.

The Earl of Iveagh, chairman of Guinness, celebrated his 80th birthday in March 1954 in the Rupert Guinness Hall, with 500 guests, and the choir of St James Musical Society provided the entertainment. He blew out the 80 candles on the 3-feet square fruit cake, weighing 70 lbs, and covered with almond and royal icing, made by Mitchels of Grafton Street.

Besides Guinness, there were other breweries in Dublin, such as Watkins Jameson Pim & Co (Ardee Street in The Coombe), and Mountjoy Brewery (Russell Street off the North Circular Road). There were also maltsters, supplying malted barley to the breweries, for example, Minch Norton (51/52 Newmarket).

Whiskey distilling was in the hands of big names, such as John Power & Son (Johns Lane Distillery – now the National College of Art & Design), and John Jameson (Bow Street Distillery – now a whiskey museum). James Hennessy were brandy distillers in 31/32 South Earl Street (Meath Street to Thomas Court).

There were some mineral-water manufacturers, such as Schweppes at 3a Mountjoy Square, and Taylor-Keith at 131 St Stephens Green.

Fitzgerald & Co, 4-5 Westmoreland Street, were classified as "Tea, wine, whiskey merchants, cordial manufacture, rectifying distillers".

Laundries & Dyers

Because nobody had a washing machine in 1954, many commercial laundries flourished, and had small branches (receiving houses) around Dublin. Big names of that era were Harold's Cross Laundry, Swastika Laundry in Ballsbridge (with their trademark symbol of peace, which was later hi-jacked by the Nazi Political Party in Germany), and Dublin Laundry in Milltown.

Smaller companies included White Swan (69a Donore Avenue), White Heather (209 South Circular Road), Kelso (103-105 Lower Rathmines Road), Dunlops (2,4,5 Mount Brown, and a few branches), Bells (cleaners & dyers), Bloomfield (13 Harcourt Road), Court (58a Harcourt Street/corner of Hatch Street), Metropolitan (61-67

Inchicore Road, Kilmainham), Cash & Carry (cleaners & dyers, 9 Nassau Street and many branches).

Many laundries were beside rivers (for a good water supply) and featured tall red-brick chimneys to serve the boilers for providing steam and hot water. Young girls were the main employees, and working conditions were damp, noisy and unpleasant.

People valued their clothes, and therefore dyed them a different colour if they fancied a change of look. Some of the laundries had dye works, such as Dartry Dye Works, owned by Dublin Laundry. Prescotts were dyers and dry-cleaners, with self-contained shops.

Dry-cleaning was coming into vogue, with such companies as Prescotts, New York Pressing Company, American Dry Cleaners (3 branches).

There were quite a few "Magdalene Laundries" around Dublin, including High Park in Drumcondra, Sean Mc Dermott Street, Stanhope Street, Goldenbridge, Leeson Street Lower, Donnybrook. These were owned and run as commercial businesses by various orders of nuns, and sometimes doubled-up as State-supported Industrial Schools for orphans or Reformatories for child offenders. So, strictly speaking, these harsh institutions did not provide employment for the public, but provided a free income for the nuns, using slave-labour.

Construction

The construction industry was a major employer, with no shortage of builders throughout Dublin. Even the big builders were based in the city centre, such as Crampton in Shelbourne Road, Ballsbridge, and Sisk in Wilton Works, 8-12 Pembroke Row, off Lower Baggot Street. In 1954, there were many interesting projects, and some are listed below.

The new Ringsend Generating Station on Pigeon House Road was being built for the Electricity Supply Board (ESB) from 1953 to 1956. This project was way before the iconic Poolbeg chimneys were built in the early 1970's.

The ESB was also building new offices on East James Street, directly behind their Georgian offices on Fitzwilliam Street Lower. The latter were demolished in the 1960's amid much controversy, and then the modern offices were themselves demolished in 2019, which just goes to prove that "modern" architecture has "built-in obsolescence", just like a car or a washing machine.

In 1954, Bolands Flour Milling Company built a new silo in Barrow Street, off Pearse Street, consisting of 30 bins of various sizes for green (fresh) and dried wheat, with a total capacity of 7,000 tons, including two large dryers. The builder was Irish Engineering and Harbour Construction Company, and the design engineer was L.G. Mouchel of London. The silo was demolished in 2016 to make way for an office/apartments development. Bolands had built a new 5-storey bakery on nearby Grand Canal Street in 1951, and their ads in 1954 included ones for sliced "Batch Loaf", thereby saving on waste from hand-cutting the bread. This well-built former bakery is now the NAMA headquarters, set up by the naive Government to enrich the American and other foreign "vulture funds" following the "Celtic Tiger" crash in 2008.

A new Electrolux vacuum-cleaner factory opened in Santry, comprising 10,000 square feet, at a cost of £35,000. The northlight space-frame roof was fabricated by J & G McGloughlin, 47-54 Pearse Street.

In January, 1954, Minister Sean Lemass opened a factory in Swords (Miltonfields) for the Textile Card Company, which manufactured machines for "carding" in the clothing industry.

A new shirt factory was built in Malpas Street, off Clanbrassil Street, for Medici Shirts Ltd, and produced 150 dozen shirts per week.

In August, a new factory was opened in Broadstone, for the assembly of David Brown farm tractors.

A new Dining Hall, serving free meals to street beggars, was opened in June at 9 Island Street (rear of Ushers Quay) by the Mendicity Institution. This charity was founded in 1818, and shortly afterwards moved to Moira House fronting on to Ushers Quay, and in 1954 included public baths/wash houses (not to be confused with swimming pools). Mrs Kelly, wife of the President of Ireland, performed the honours for the £11,000 Dining Hall project. The rear Dining Hall still serves daily meals, but the front site of Moira House is now occupied by a 1960'S office block occupied by the HSE.

April 1954 saw the opening and church blessing of the new "State Cinema" for Odeon Cinemas (built by Irish Estates Ltd, 41 Mespil Road for £100,000), on the site of the impressive Phibsboro Cinema, built in 1914 at 376 North Circular Road (near Doyles Corner). This new "state-of-the-art" cinema, held 1,300 patrons, had a "wide-screen", and was air-conditioned. The first show at 8pm was "West of Zanzibar". Unable to compete with the attractions of the new-fangled television, the cinema closed in 1974. Recently, the building was used as a Des Kelly interiors-furniture shop, and is nowadays for sale as part of a development site. Besides the new State cinema, this suburb also had the Bohemian Picture Theatre at 154/155 Phibsborough Road.

The 1,500-seater "Whitehall Grand" cinema opened in July, 1954, and there were five other cinemas under construction in that year – Ballyfermot, Dundrum, Mount Merrion, Stillorgan, Finglas.

In January, Archbishop McQuaid laid the foundation-stone for a new 3-storey Baldoyle Orthopaedic Hospital, which dealt with infantile paralysis, and was run by the Sisters of Charity, although funded by the Government. The original hospital had opened in 1943. That same month, the foundation stone was laid at the Meath Hospital for a new Urological Department (genito-urinary problems).

In September, a new 80-bed two-storey Maternity Hospital was opened and blessed in St Kevins Hospital, James Street, and a new X-Ray department also opened in that year. St Kevins was originally built as the Workhouse, also known as the South Dublin Union (featuring in the 1916 Easter Rising), and was later renamed St James Hospital, nowadays a huge campus, and will soon incorporate the €2billion National Childrens Hospital currently under construction.

In October, a new Outpatients Department opened in the Royal City of Dublin Hospital in Baggot Street Upper, including 23 bedrooms for nurses on the 1st and 2nd floors.

The new St Lukes Cancer Hospital opened in 1954 in Highfield Road, Rathgar, where it is still based.

The new 5,200-seater stand was under construction in Lansdowne Road, Ballsbridge, home of Irish rugby.

Dublin Corporation was engaged in the construction of the Dolphins Barn low-rise blocks of council-flats (now called "social housing") alongside the attractive Grand Canal.

Builders-Providers

T. & C. Martin were big builders-providers based in 21-24 D'Olier Street, (D'Olier House) right beside The Red Bank Restaurant. Mother Mary Martin, founder of the Medical Missionaries of Mary in Drogheda in 1938, was one of the wealthy Martin family. In previous decades, the site was the Junior Army & Navy Stores, similar to McBirneys and other general department stores, but was rebuilt by G & T Crampton in 1926 for the Martin business. Now a modern office block, D'Olier House, is on the site. Like other builders-providers, T & C Martin had timber stock yards and warehouses on the north docklands.

Brooks Thomas, another big builders-providers, had a large premises in Lower Abbey Street, where the Irish Life Headquarters was built in 1980, and a retail outlet at 4 Sackville Place. They were stockists of Crittal Steel Windows, which were all the rage then, and Westmoreland Green Quarry Slates (slightly green in colour) from Broughton Moor quarries, near Coniston, Cumbria, England.

Thomas Dockrell Sons & Co Ltd were in 38/39 Georges Street, being also a major hardware store.

Other companies included Glorneys in Moss Street, Heitons at 32-37 Georges Quay (they were also coal merchants), McFerran & Guilford in Tara Street, Chadwicks in Talbot Place, Ruberoid Roofing (bitumen felt), Holroyd & Jones in 14 Princess Street (also stocked formica), Monsell Mitchell & Co in Townsend Street (sanitary ware), Walpamur Paint Manufacturing in 9-12 Cardiff Lane, MRCB in Lord Edward Street (paint stockists), Joseph Kelly sawmills at 67-68 Thomas Street (nowadays a Chadwicks Builders Providers), Baxendale in Capel Street.

Kennan & Sons, 16-20 Fishamble Street, specialised in steel fabrications, including fencing and railings. Next door was Dublin Corporation Waterworks Department, occupying the Old Music Hall site where Handel's "Messiah" was first performed in 1742.

Bread and Flour

The big commercial bakeries supplied bread to various bread-shops around the city, and also to many Dublin households, using electric vans crawling from door to door with fresh bread daily. The big names included Johnstons, Mooney & O'Brien (Ballsbridge bakery, and Clonliffe Mills, 28a Jones Road, alongside Croke Park), Bolands (Pearse Street Flour Mill and nearby Grand Canal Street bakery).

Peter Kennedy Bakers at 124-131 Parnell Street, also operated a few restaurants and coffee shops, trading as the Dublin Bread Company, (27 Stephens Street Lower, 38 St Stephens Green, and 173 Lower Rathmines Road).

Jacobs in Bishop Street (now partly the National Archives) was more famous for its biscuits.

Sweets & Chocolate

Dublin abounded in sweet factories in 1954, catering all year round to the non-stop needs of little children craving cheap sweets, and big children requiring expensive chocolates. Christmas was the time for big boxes of the goodies to be mass-produced.

Children sucked and chewed tons of hard boiled sweets such as "Acid Drops", "Bulls Eyes", "Clove Drops", and cheap toffee bars (black liquorice or brown), and "gob-stoppers" the size of plums.

Cleeves was a milk-processing company based in Limerick from 1927, and also became famous amongst wealthy children for their Cleeves luxury cream toffee bars (in brown slabs of squares pieces). The toffee factory was in McKee Avenue, Finglas, when they closed in 1985.

Fox's Glazier Mints (wrapped boiled sweets) were made at 6 Parkview, off Westland Row.

Lemons Pure Sweets had the factory at Millmount Place, Drumcondra, and a sweet shop called "The Confectioners Hall" in 49 Lower O'Connell Street.

Clarnico Murray had their sweet factory at Mount Tallant Avenue in Harold's Cross, producing such items as Nougat Rolls (individually wrapped sweets) at 9d a quarter pound, Iced Caramels at 9d a quarter, Bridesmaid Caramels at 1/- a quarter, and Regency Candies.

Maynards Wine Gums were made by J.M. Gargan & Co, 51 Middle Abbey Street, and cost 10/½ a quarter.

Urneys was a big chocolate factory in Tallaght, making such items as Milk Tray bars for 3d, Festive Assortment chocolates at 11d a quarter, Café-Au-Lait bars, Cream Bars for 3d, Turkish Delight at 3d a bar, or boxes of Royal chocolates, in 1lb and 2 lb boxes, at 6/- a pound.

Rowntree had their chocolate factory opposite Kilmainham Jail at 34-38 Inchicore Road. They later amalgamated with Mackintosh of Rathmines Road Lower. Rowntree produced Aero bars and Kit-Kat bars, both at 5d, and small tubes of Smarties for 4d. Mackintosh made Rolo sweets, and also "Double Centre" chocolate toffee assortment.

Fry-Cadbury had their chocolate factory at 74-112 East Wall Road, and also Ossary Road, making Cadburys "Dairy Milk" and Frys "Milk Punch", both 4d a bar.

Besides their famous "Cream Cracker" biscuits and "Fig Roll" biscuits, Jacobs also made "Patricia" chocolates, selling at 6/- for a lb.

Lamb Bros on the Naas Road in Inchicore were famous for jams, especially the "Fruitfield" brand, growing the fruit on their own farms around Dublin county, employing hundreds of young casual workers in the Summer picking season.

Williams & Woods, 204 Parnell Street/22-26 Kings Inns Street, were famous for jams, and also made sweets.

Tobacco

There was an official report in 1953 stating that smoking causes lung cancer, yet still a large number of men smoked a pipe as a prestige symbol, and to stop their hands fidgeting in public places. But cigarettes (mostly un-tipped/unfiltered until the 1960's) were starting to become fashionable and very addictive.

Kapp & Peterson, were the leading manufacturers and retailers of clay pipes and accessories, with their factory and offices at 113 St Stephens Green (north of Unitarian Church), and retail shops at both 55 & 117 Grafton Street, and both 2 & 56 Lower O'Connell Street (the latter had a big neon sign on its façade). Pipe tobacco was available in loose form in small circular tins, and also in little blocks, the latter costing 2/9 an ounce, with such brands as St Bruno, Yachtsman, and Odgens (the latter made by the Imperial Tobacco Company).

P. J. Carroll, Dundalk, manufactured "Sweet Afton" and "Carrolls No 1" cigarettes, and also produced very expensive cigars for Christmas – such as a box of twelve "La Hermosa Sublimes" for 30/-.

John Player & Sons had their cigarette factory at 57-75 Botanic Road, Glasnevin, beside Alexander Thoms printing works (Iona Works). The front offices had a lovely granite facade, with their "JP&S" shield over the entrance. Their famous neon advertising signs "Players Please" were on various buildings around the city centre, suggesting that pleasure can be derived from smoking Players cigarettes, and also to be mannerly in shops when choosing a packet of cigarettes (please give me a packet of Players cigarettes). "Navy Cut" was their most famous brand. During the "Tostal" national festival in the Spring of 1954, Players were selling boxes of 50 cigarettes for 5/10, wrapped in special Tostal paper.

The Wills cigarette factory was at 148-160 South Circular Road, Dolphins Barn, and was a subsidiary of the Imperial Tobacco Company of Great Britain & Ireland. They manufactured "Gold Flake" and "Woodbine" brands, a packet of ten costing 1/- (one shilling).

John Player and Wills amalgamated in the 1960's, to create Player Wills, retaining only the factory at Dolphins Barn. Later, the company sponsored the talent competition entitled "John Player Tops of the Town", and the cigarette company even built the comfortable John Player Theatre beside their factory.

The Astor tobacco company was originally at 8/9 Fownes Street, off Dame Street, and in April, 1954, their new factory opened at 285 Cashel Road, Kimmage. The 45,00 square feet building, including a worker's canteen, was designed by Joseph Kidney and built by G & T Crampton, featuring a large bow-shaped stairwell for the two-storey office section, and even had double-glazed windows. Their cigarettes were mostly exported, including State Express 333, State Express 555, State Express 777, and Double Ace. Christmas boxes of 50 State Express 555 sold for 7/4, 75 for 11/-, 100 for 14/7, and 200 for 29/2 (£1.9.2). For some unknown reason, the Astor cigarette factory lasted only for about four years, and was sold in 1958 to Leo Laboratories, nowadays trading as Leo Pharma on the same site.

"Have you got a light, mister" was a well-known question beloved of penniless young "gurriers" and "guttersnipes" throughout Dublin, in order to light the single cigarette they had bought in a corner shop, or even the small cigarette butt they had picked up in the gutter. Therefore, a little box of matches was an essential component of serious pipe and cigarette smoking, often made by Maguire & Paterson in their factories at 4-5 Bow Street, and 170-177 Church Street.

Coras Iompair Eireann (CIE)

Besides hundreds of bus and train drivers, the vast CIE Inchicore Works employed 1,200 - 1,400 skilled men such as mechanics, carpenters, fitters etc, in making train carriages, repairing engines, etc.

Domestics

Most middle-class homes in Dublin employed at least one female maid, known as "domestic help", who lived with the family, and slept in the smallest room in the house, despite the fact that the mother did not go out to work. Even the lower-middle classes strove for this "badge of distinction". The market for domestics was partly fuelled by the output of the State-supported convent-run Industrial Schools and Reformatories.

Miscellaneous

In July, 1954, Tonge & Taggart ironfoundry of 10 Windmill Lane and East Wall Road amalgamated with J & G McGloughlin of 47-54 Pearse Street - the latter were big in structural steelwork fabrication and erection.

Amongst other employers in Dublin were Smith & Pearson steel windows, Unidare factory in Finglas, Frigidaire at 75 Cork Street (fridges, Hoover vacuum cleaners and washing machines), Rathbourne candles at 132 East Wall Road, Lalor candles at 14 Lower Ormond Quay, Britvic Tomato Cocktail (non-alcoholic) in Crumlin, Paul & Vincent at 9-13 Blackhall Place and 80-81 Sir John Rogersons Quay (fertiliser, animal feeds), Donnelly in Cork Street (sausages and rashers), Ferrier Pollock clothing, 59 South William Street (Powerscourt House), Kileen Paper Mills at Inchicore, Sunbeam Wolsey hosiery at 39-45 South King Street (and Millfield Cork), Gaelite Neon Signs at 6,7,8 Magennis Place, off Pearse Street, Taylor Neon Signs on Grove Road, Portobello, Ever-Ready dry batteries in Portobello Harbour (the older "wet batteries" had to be re-charged in a shop), Bailey & Gibson at South Circular Road, beside Wills cigarettes (paper manufacture and printers).

There were many clothing factories in small premises around Dublin, in back streets and above shops, sometimes known as "sweat shops", and often the preserve of the Jewish community.

Manufacturing chemists were also numerous, with some big firms such as Boileau & Boyd at 88-93 Bride Street, and Aspro on the Naas Road in Bluebell.

Specialist artists found employment opportunities in firms such as "The Tower of Glass" (An Tur Gloine) situated at the rear of 24/25 Upper Pembroke Street (rear of the Grey Door Hotel), which was still under the control of Catherine O'Brien in 1954, and was in the process of making a stained-glass window by Patrick Pollon. Earley & Company of 4/5 Upper Camden Street, were sculptors and stained-glass artists. The Dun Emer Guild of craftworkers were in 41 Harcourt Street. John A. Deghini & Sons, 1-3 Lower Exchange Street, were kept busy making statues of Our Lady (Mary) for the Marian Year, as were Harrisons, 175-178 Pearse Street.

Unemployment

The State unemployment benefit ("dole") in 1954 was 38/- per week (28/- for rural dwellers), for a married couple with two or more children. The womens "labour exchange", for collecting the weekly cash, was at Victoria Street in Portobello, while the mens was in Werburgh Street nearly opposite Burdocks "chipper", and 50 Lower Gardiner Street (behind Brooks Thomas builders providers). An Roinn Slainte (Department of Health) paid a Disabled Persons Allowance of about £1 a week.

In 1954, Richard Atkinson & Co, world-famous poplin manufactures (dresses, mens ties), which had been founded by Huguenots (French Protestants) in Dublin in 1820, closed their Dublin factory, although it was only built in 1949. The 20,000 square feet factory, on a 14-acre site in Swords, had employed 45 weavers. Their Belfast premises, which handled exports to Canada, was not affected.

For those unable to find productive employment, the Irish Army placed glamorous advertisements in the national newspapers seeking recruits, and even listing the rates of pay and allowances.

The Labour Court was based in part of Griffith Barracks on the South Circular Road, and handled a dispute concerning which tradesmen should be engaged to build lightweight passenger train coaches at the CIE Inchicore Works.

Trade Promotion

The Institute for Research & Standards was based in Glasnevin House, promoting good standards in manufacturing. The Industrial Development Authority (IDA) had offices in 14 St Stephens Green, helping businesses to set up factories. There was also a Permanent Exhibition of Irish Manufacturers in 3 St Stephens Green.

The original Central Bank in Foster Place was part of the former Irish Parliament premises, and is now the Stock Exchange.

There were hundreds of dock-workers in the 1950's.
(Courtesy of Dublin City Library & Archives).

The Rupert Guinness Theatre on Watling Street is still standing.

G. A. Brittain car-assembly works for the popular Morris Minor was beside Portobello Bridge, and the site is now in housing and office use.

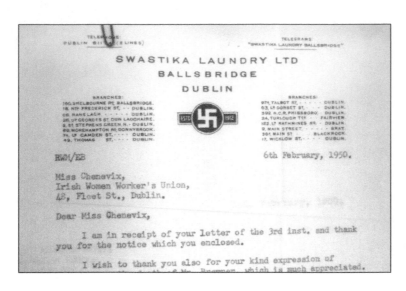

SWASTIKA LAUNDRY LTD
BALLSBRIDGE
DUBLIN

RWM/EB   6th February, 1950.

Miss Chenevix,
Irish Women Worker's Union,
48, Fleet St., Dublin.

Dear Miss Chenevix,

I am in receipt of your letter of the 3rd inst. and thank you for the notice which you enclosed.

I wish to thank you also for your kind expression of

The Swastika Laundry had nothing to do with the German Nazi Party.

Williams & Woods sweet factory on Kings Inns Street is still standing.

The original Wills cigarette factory (later called Player Wills) in Dolphins Barn, is awaiting re-development.

The original John Player cigarette factory in Glasnevin awaits re-development.

This 1954 Mendicity Institution dining room behind Ushers Quay is still active.

Only the railings and piers remain of the Mendicity Institution on Ushers Quay.

Health

Hospitals

Dublin was well supplied with hospitals, most dating from the Georgian and Victorian eras, founded by wealthy citizens, and some owned or managed by nuns. Most hospitals had dispensaries/out-patients departments.

There were three maternity hospitals, Rotunda, Holles Street, and the Coombe (the latter was relocated to nearby Dolphins Barn in 1967).

The Meath Hospital & County Dublin Infirmary on Heytesbury Street, and the National Childrens Hospital on 86-89 Harcourt Street, both relocated to Tallaght Hospital in 1998, as did the Adelaide Hospital on Peter Street, the latter under Protestant control.

St Vincents Hospital on St Stephens Green, owned and run by the Sisters of Charity, moved to Elm Park in Merrion in 1970. Their St Winifreds Private Hospital was at 93/94 Lower Leeson Street. Hume Street skin hospital moved to St Vincents in 2006.

St Kevins Hospital, which was originally the South Dublin Union Workhouse, and included the Rialto Chest Hospital for Tuberculosis (TB) up to 1957 (at 148 South Circular Road), was renamed as St James Hospital in the 1970's. The Royal City of Dublin Hospital on Upper Baggot Street moved to St James in the 1980's, as did Sir Patrick Duns Hospital on Grand Canal Street Lower, and the Mercer Hospital.

Dr Steevens Hospital closed in 1987, and is now the Health Service Executive (HSE) headquarters, but St Patricks Hospital for Mental Diseases (Swifts Hospital) directly behind, is still open.

St Ultans Infant Hospital on 36/37 Charlemont Street transferred to Harcourt Street Childrens hospital in 1984. In Crumlin, Our Ladys Hospital for Sick Children, with 308 beds, which was built on church land in the early 1950's, officially opened in November 1956, and was run for Archbishop McQuaid by the Sisters of Charity of St Vincent de Paul.

Cherry Orchard Fever Hospital opened in 1953, taking patients from Cork Street Fever Hospital. St Lukes Cancer Hospital on Highfield Road in Rathgar opened in phases between 1951 and 1954. The Royal Victoria Eye & Ear Hospital is still on Adelaide Road, and its rear dispensary supplied spectacles to the public, including children.

St Margaret of Cortona Hospital was in 22-23 Townsend Street until 1956, although was known until 1946 as the Westmoreland Lock Hospital, dealing only with cases of venereal disease in women, mostly prostitutes who "plied their trade " in the nearby grubby docklands around Sir John Rogersons Quay. Samuel Lewis, writing in 1837, states that it opened in 1792 for Venereal Disease in male and female patients, although other sources state that it was actually extended on that date. The building was essentially "H" shaped, being two-storey over basement at the front, and three storey at the rear. The front was enhanced by a single storey wing on both sides. In the 18th century, there was a hospital on this site known as St Margaret of Cortona or the Hospital for Incurables. The site is now occupied by College Gate modern apartments behind the modern Irish Times office block.

The Dental Hospital at 23-28 Lincoln Place is still in operation. In the 1950's, children used the free dental clinic in 10-14 Cornmarket (near Johns Lane church) operated by Dublin Corporation.

North of the River Liffey, Jervis Street Hospital (founded 1718, and rebuilt on a larger scale in 1885) was run by the Sisters of Mercy, and transferred to the new Beaumont Hospital in Whitehall in 1987. In North Brunswick Street, St Laurences Hospital (originally three separate institutions: Richmond Surgical, Whitworth Medical, and Hardwicke Fever Hospital) survived until 1987 before moving to Beaumont Hospital.

The Mater Hospital, run by the Sisters of Mercy, is still thriving, including their Private Hospital started in 1924. Their College of Nursing opened in July 1954. The State-owned Voluntary Health Insurance (VHI) was not set up until 1957, and only rich patients could afford private hospital treatment before that year.

St Josephs Childrens Hospital in Temple Street, is still owned by the Sisters of Charity.

St Brendans Psychiatric Hospital in Grangegorman is now a Third Level Institution, after the remaining patients were transferred to Portrane Hospital in recent decades.

St Marys Chest Hospital in the Phoenix Park, was an Army Hospital during World War Two, and a Military Academy for young boys before that, and is now a Nursing Home.

St Bricans Army Hospital, Infirmary Road, is still open. In the 1950's, the nurses wore their Army uniform when in public places.

Our Ladys Hospital for the Dying in Harold's Cross is now larger than ever, but is no longer the preserve of terminally-ill patients.

Dublin had other smaller hospitals, in addition to some hospitals in the county areas, including St Annes in Northbrook Road, Ranelagh (skin & cancer), St Marys Childrens Sanatorium in Cappagh, Peamount Tuberculosis (TB) Sanatorium.

The National Blood Transfusion Association, 52 Lower Leeson Street (they later moved to nearby Mespil Road), was founded in 1950, but they were more commonly known as the Blood Bank, and their offices were known as Pelican House. In December 1954, they showed a promotional film in the Gresham Hotel, entitled "It's in the Bank", and reminded the public that hospitals needed 500 units of blood per week, and that their mobile unit could accept donations of blood from the general public.

Nurses in the 1950's wore a white shoulder-length linen veil, and most nurses lived in Nurses Homes on the hospital grounds. Photos of nurses often featured in the newspapers, for example, during 1954, nurses in the Rotunda Maternity Hospital singing Christmas Carols for their patients, Prize Day in the Adelaide Hospital (11th June), annual distribution of nurses prizes in St Vincents Hospital by Archbishop McQuaid (e.g. the Magennis Medal), photo in April of a group of trained nurses on a ten-day refresher course in Jervis Street Hospital.

In 1952, Lady Valerie Goulding (wife of Basil Goulding of 10:10:20 fertiliser fame) started the Central Remedial Clinic for post-hospital treatment of infantile paralysis, in 16 Upper Pembroke Street, using volunteer drivers to collect the child patients and bring them home again later in the day. In 1954, she bought Prospect Hall, a 20-room mansion (2-storey over basement with two wings) in Goatstown, and at that time was treating up to 400 child outpatients annually for polio and orthopaedic cases. The Clinic is nowadays headquartered in Clontarf.

In 1954, a new childrens Sunshine Home opened in Stillorgan (the old one was built 1925), an initiative of Miss Letitia Everend of Airfield in Dundrum, and catered for mild rickets, coeliac disease, and post-pneumatic debility.

In 1954, "Dunfillan House" on Orwell Road in Rathgar was sold to the St John of God Brothers, who set up their Child Guidance Clinic, specialising in speech therapy.

St Johns Ambulance Brigade had a First Aid Hut in the central reservation on O'Connell Street Upper (opposite the Carlton cinema), which treated about 400 cases a year. What do shoppers do nowadays?

Other Health Matters

There was a Public Enquiry in October 1954 into the proposal to close St James Cemetery, James Street, because of overcrowding. Thereafter the cemetery, with Catholic and Protestant graves, became badly run-down, until a few years ago when the front Protestant Church was converted into Pierce Lyons distillery, and the rear graveyard partly cleaned-up.

Unlike nowadays, the public was well served by semi-basement Public Toilets, in such useful locations as the central reservation in Upper O'Connell Street (opposite the Savoy cinema), College Street and Westmoreland Street junction, Kevin Street and Patrick Street junction, St Stephens Green West (fully above ground). There was a dedicated Ladies Toilet on Burgh Quay, beside the Quay wall adjacent to O'Connell Bridge.

The former Richmond Hospital on North Brunswick Street was recently a District Court, and is now offices.

The semi-basement public toilet at Kevin Street/Patrick Street, is now abandoned, yet the need is now greater than ever.

The Ladies public toilet on Burgh Quay no longer exists. Note the public telephone box, and also the Corinthian Cinema on the opposite Eden Quay, all now gone. (Courtesy of Dublin City Library & Archives).

Peace & Justice

Law Courts

In 1954, court barristers wore horse-hair wigs, extending down both sides of their head to their chest, and twin white strips of cloth instead of a tie.

The judges and barristers attended their "Votive Mass" in St Michans Catholic Church, Halston Street, at the opening of the Michaelmas Law Term. This Law Term started on 1st October, with the upcoming cases listed in the newspapers.

In November there was a Supreme Court Appeal against a failed High Court libel action for £500 commenced in February by Patrick Kavanagh, poet and journalist, of Pembroke Road, Ballsbridge, against The Leader newspaper, Drogheda, and their printer. The following March the High Court decision was overturned, because the original "learned" judge had misdirected the jury, but worn-out Kavanagh accepted an un-known out-of-Court settlement, instead of a new High Court action.

During the year, Batchelor & Co, based in Cabra West, was involved in a dispute with the Lower Prices Council, concerning peas. 23,000 packets of peas had been seized by Gardai, but returned later.

In December 1954, the owners of the Pillar Ice Cream Parlour and Pillar Casino Amusements at 62 Upper O'Connell Street were charged in Dublin District Court with showing an indecent exhibition amongst the forty slot machines on the first floor – a slot machine with stills (photographs) of nude and semi-nude females, costing 1d to see seven stills. The Senezio family, who started their business here in 1945, were fined £40.

There was another Court case in December, involving a garage at the rear of 340 Harold's Cross Road, which was being used to show an indecent film for profit (presumably there would be no crime if punters were admitted free-of-charge!).

Garda Siochana (Police)

Even in the 1950's, the Irish Times newspaper never referred to the Garda Siochana (Irish for "Guardians of the Peace"), only reporting on the activities of the Civic Guard, despite the fact that the latter name was only in existence from 1922 to 1923.

In the mid-1950's, new male Gardai (no females until 1959) were trained in the "Depot" in the Phoenix Park, the former headquarters of the Royal Irish Constabulary (RIC). Templemore Army Barracks in Co Tipperary was vacated after the Second World War, and then used as training grounds by the FCA (reserve army) up to 1964, when it was converted into the Garda Training College. The former Royal Hospital Kilmainham was also used by the Garda Siochana for a few decades after 1922 as their offices, before moving back to the Depot in the Phoenix Park, after which the Board of Works (later called the Office of Public Works) used the former Hospital partly as a store, but it mostly lay empty and neglected for decades.

In April, 1954, 251 new recruits were in the "Passing-Out" parade at the Depot, Phoenix Park, after their six months training. That year, the total police force for Ireland was 6,642, including 1,641 in Dublin. Dublin police wore a collar and tie, whereas rural police had old-style high-neck tunics.

In June, the Gardai bought a small fleet of Vauxhall Velox saloons from McCairns Motors, bringing the total in Ireland to 200 squad cars, of different manufacture, and each was fitted with Lucas radio equipment. Motor cycle traffic police had been launched in Dublin in April 1953, and some rural Garda stations were provided with slower scooters. The public's retrieved stolen bicycles were stored in Kevin Street Garda Station, and any un-claimed ones were auctioned off cheaply once a year, when penniless students could bag a bargain.

Crime

Dublin had its share of troublemakers, and the evening newspapers reported on a lot of petty crime and minor Court cases. The Evening

Herald reported that on the 14th October, 1954, Garda James Christopher Branigan (nick-named "Lugs" because of his big ears) attended two big street fights around Patrick Street and Longford Row, where up to 300 drunk men were brawling after close of numerous local pubs between 12midnight and 1am.

On New Years Eve 1954, the boisterous crowd at Christ Church Cathedral was baton-charged by the Gardai, and five people were hurt. The famous bells had stopped at 12.15 am on 1/1/55, but the crowd continued to sing and dance. That same night, the Fire-Brigade was called out six times to bonfires, especially in Whitehall, Larkhill, and Beggars Bush.

There were the "Animal Gangs" in the 1940's, who engaged in vicious faction-fights with rival gangs, but these were dealt with by "Lugs Branigan", who mopped them up in the usual "Black Mariah" (a black van) and a "good clip on their ears" or a "foot in the pants". The "Teddy Boys" appeared around 1954, but were less trouble to Lugs.

In December, 9-month old Patrick Berrigan was stolen from his pram in Henry Street, and found unharmed five days later in the care of a lonely women in Belfast. Another baby had been stolen in Camden Street on the 19th October, but local police were still searching in Belfast in December.

An unusual and probably unique crime took place in November, when 4 cwt of ornamented bronze gunmetal was stolen from the base of the Wellington Monument in the Phoenix Park, but was later recovered and the culprit brought to Court.

Prisons

On the 20th April, 1954, 25-year old Michael Manning was the last person to be hanged in Ireland, following his conviction for the murder of elderly Catherine Cooper in Limerick. The rare event took place in Mountjoy Jail, and Albert Pierrepoint from England was the hangman.

In the 1950's, the historic Kilmainham Jail, where the 1916 Easter Rising leaders were executed by the British army, lay empty and dilapidated, and it wasn't until 1960 that patriotic volunteers started a slow restoration. Nowadays, the State runs a museum in the building.

Army

In the 19th century, the British had built many army barracks throughout Ireland, in order to force the Irish people into submission following various insurrections, generally employing wealthy Irish Protestants as senior officers, and many poor Irish men as army privates. These barracks were taken over by the new Irish Army following Independence in 1922, and were retained to stem any Anti-Treaty activities. In 1954, there were still a lot of Irish Army barracks around Dublin (and Ireland), and actively recruiting innocent lads, via glamorous advertisements in the national newspapers, one such ad showing a recruit playing football with the Army team. As a result, Dublin was teeming with army privates dressed in full uniform, wandering around in their free time and frequenting the numerous pubs. The FCA Army Reserve also provided a good supply of lads strolling around showing off their green uniforms to admiring teenage girls. Nowadays, Collins Barracks is the National Museum (although the accommodation is most unsuitable), Griffith Barracks is a Third-level college, Islandbridge/Clancy Barracks is an estate of apartments, part of Cathal Brugha Barracks has been sold off, and Beggars Bush is now commercial offices, social housing, and private dwellings.

The Army held an open-air Mass for St Patricks Day, outside St Patricks Garrison Church in Cathal Brugha Barracks, Rathmines, which could be watched by the public from the Grand Canal entrance on Grove Road.

There was a photograph in the Irish Independent in June of the Survey Company, Corps of Engineers, at the Ordnance Survey offices in the Phoenix Park, where the first group of 26 army men received their certificates in surveying after completing the 3-year training course.

Rural Ireland

Religion

"Hours of Dancing in Ardagh" ran a newspaper headline in October 1954, referring to a meeting of dance-hall owners from Longford and Leitrim, presided over by the Bishop, when they agreed to abide by Diocesan Regulations, i.e. dancing allowed up to 1am in Summer, and 12 midnight in Winter.

As a change from Marian Statues, the Statue of St Barbara, patron saint of gunners, was unveiled and blessed by the Bishop on the 5th April, 1954, in Magee Barracks, Hospital Street, Kildare town, for the Irish Army Artillery Corps. This barracks is now closed, and the statue was re-erected in Plunkett Barracks on the Curragh in 1999.

On 16th May, 3,000 pilgrims converged on Drogheda to visit the Blessed Oliver Plunkett shrine in St Peters Church, West Street. Another 6,000 were in attendance on the 11th July.

On the 22nd August, a 45-foot tall cross, Christ the King, was erected on the Devils Bit Mountain, near Cashel in County Tipperary, although it was a pity that a statue of Our Lady was not chosen for the Marian Year, instead of a very plain concrete edifice.

New Churches & Schools

The clergy blessed the new Oratory in the Convent of Mercy, Castlerea, County Roscommon. The main contractor was J.J. Rhatigan of Milltown, Tuam, while the coffered plaster ceiling was by M. Creedon of South Richmond Place in Dublin, and the hardwood wood-block floors were provided by James McMahon of Limerick.

In Ballybricken, County Waterford, the new Church of the Holy Family was opened in April, at a cost of £115,000, and the architects presented a gold key to the parish.

In March, a new church dedicated to the Immaculate Conception was officially opened in Lahinch, County Clare.

On 27th May, the foundation stone was laid for the new Church of the Immaculate Conception in Belturbet, County Cavan, accompanied by a big Marian Procession around the town. The new building, which is situated beside the imposing Anglican Church, cost £50,000, could accommodate 1,120 people, and was officially opened on 3rd October (Rosary Sunday) by celebrating High Mass in the old St Marys Church.

On the 15th August, the new Church of the Immaculate Conception opened at Allenwood, County Kildare, which was intended to cater for the new Bord na Mona nearby village of Coill Dubh (Blackwood). The old village had used a "tin church" (prefabricated) for 50 years, and the new church was built with free local labour.

On the 28th October, the new Church of the Immaculate Conception was opened at Filemore (Foilmore), a remote region east of Cahersiveen in Kerry, because the old one was in bad repair.

In Doonaha, near Kilkee, County Clare, the old Penal church was rebuilt, thus preserving the historic built heritage for generations to come.

Archbishop McQuaid opened the new Technical School (Tech) in Wicklow town in February.

New National Schools were opened in both Dunshaughlin and Ashbourne in County Meath.

On the 19th October, the new St Patricks Boys National School opened at Bothar Brugha, Drogheda, County Louth, and the bill was £20,000 for the 7-classroom building, catering for 300 boys (43 boys in each room). The new St Brigids National School will hold 400 girls, and cost £45,000. On the 25th October, the new National School for the Sisters of Mercy opened in Dundalk, County Louth, catering for 600 girls, at a cost of £80,000 (which was very expensive)

On the 7th November, the new Christian Brothers School (CBS) opened in Naas, County Kildare, catering for 350 boys.

Fr Peyton

Fr Patrick Peyton was born in 1909 in Attymass, a tiny village between Ballina and Foxford in County Mayo. At the age of nineteen, he emigrated to America, and later joined the Congregation of Holy Cross.

In the 1940's, he became devoted to reciting the "Rosary" (a decade of the Rosary means one "Our Father", "Hail Mary" ten times, and one "Glory Be to the Father"), and encouraged families to do likewise, his motto being: "The family that prays together, stays together." In America he harnessed the power of radio and television to promote the Rosary, enlisting Hollywood stars in his campaigns, and over the next three decades held big rallies all around the world, and enjoyed a "jet-set lifestyle", apparently part-funded by the American Central intelligence Agency (CIA) in its campaigns against the spread of Communism.

1954 was the year that Fr Peyton came to Ireland, where he attended twenty-one big Family Rosary Crusade rallies. Starting on the 25th April in the Tuam GAA Stadium, County Galway, some of the other rallies included Knock Shrine on the 2nd May (18,000 attended Mass at the Apparition Oratory, with many invalids in wheelchairs and on stretchers), Ballybrit Racecourse in Galway (30,000), Loughrea in County Galway, Ballaghadereen in County Roscommon, Sligo Showgrounds (20,000), James Stephens Park in Ballina, Co Mayo (15,000), Cusack Park in Mullingar (17,000).

In June, 4,000 people listened to Fr Peyton at a temporary altar in The Square, Belmullet, Co Mayo, where a statue of the Blessed Virgin was paraded through the town, people knelt as the procession passed their houses, and blue and white flags were displayed in honour of Our Lady.

Later in June, 15,000 people attended the Peyton Rosary Rally in Pairc Tailteann (GAA grounds), in Navan, County Meath, where there were flags and bunting, and miniature altars and shrines in house windows. The Procession started at St Marys Church, consisting of clergy, school children, Children of Mary Sodality in their blue lace veils, FCA, Order of Malta, the public in their "Sunday Best", all reciting the Rosary aloud along the way, accompanied by hymn-singing over the temporary loud-speakers on the lamp-posts, and then celebrating Benediction in the GAA grounds.

The 15th August, 1954, was the final rally (21st) of Fr Peyton at Our Ladys Island in Wexford, with 40,000 in attendance. Later, the national newspapers had a photo Fr Peyton leaving Dublin Airport, bound for Spain and more mass rallies, and then on to India and Africa, before returning to America.

Farming

Ireland had a good cattle export business in 1954, generally to England, and herd sizes had increased since artificial-insemination (AI) had been introduced in 1946. In order to preserve this valuable industry, the bovine tuberculosis (bovine TB) eradication scheme started in September 1954, initially amongst cattle herds in the west of Ireland, and then extending to other parts of the country in the following years.

Rabbits were a big food business in Ireland, and were also exported to England. Even their skins were valuable as furs, and used as expensive clothing accessories. Rabbits were slightly cheaper to buy than chickens, and cost nothing to feed. Then the disease of myxomatosis hit them in 1954, wiping out the industry very quickly.

Since 1933, Comhlucht Siuicre Eireann (Irish Sugar Company), based in 7 Clare Street in Dublin, was the State company responsible for the production of sugar in Ireland, and about 72,000 acres of land were used by a large number of farmers for growing the sugar beet (which looked like a turnip)), which was then processed in the factories in Carlow, Mallow, Thurles and Tuam. In 1954, the price of sugar beet was fixed at 108/- (£5/8/0) per ton, for beet with a 15% sugar content.

In 1954, a combined total of 10,000 acres of land in the south-east of Ireland was used as apple-orchards, regarded as a great money-making crop. No doubt, some of the apples ended up in Clonmel, where Magner (Bulmers) produced Cidona and Cider.

Lamb Bros, makers of jam and marmalade, who grew their own strawberries and raspberries on their 400 acre farms at Beaverstown in Donabate, County Dublin, employed 500 workers seasonally in Summer (young women and children).

In November, the Goffs Bloodstock Sales (valuable horses) took place in the RDS in Ballsbridge. The company moved to Kildare in the 1970's, and now have an international reputation.

Many farmhouses in rural Ireland had no electricity, and instead relied on paraffin oil (Aladdin Pink), supplied by Irish Shell Ltd, for lighting, heating and cooking. The ESB's "Rural Electrification Scheme" started in 1947, and was expected to finish around 1960. In some houses, the owners were terrified of this new-fangled invention, but might have reluctantly agreed to the provision of one light bulb in the hallway, and maybe one single socket in the kitchen!

Most farmers welcomed the modern lightweight steel-framed haybarns, and Patrick Kelly & Co of Portlaoise were one of the main suppliers and erectors. Their barns were 22 ft or 25 ft wide, and 30ft, 45ft, 60ft or 75ft long. The sides and ends could be part-sheeted with galvanised corrugated steel (heavy-gauge pre-War quality), 6ft, 8ft, or 10ft high. Long-term loans were available from the State-owned Agricultural Credit Corporation, and free grants up to £75 were provided by the Dept of Agriculture. Smith & Pearson also supplied and erected similar hay barns.

Agricultural Shows

The National Ploughing Championship was held in Cahir (County Tipperary) in February, and Ronald Sheane of Kilbride, Co Wicklow, was chosen to represent Ireland in the World Ploughing Contest which took place in October in Killarney, County Kerry (St Fintans Mental Hospital Grounds at Gortroe), and was sponsored by Esso Oil. From a field of thirteen countries, 28-year old Hugh Barr from Coleraine, Northern Ireland, was the winner, driving a Fordson Major Diesel tractor. The prizes were presented in the Great Southern Hotel, Killarney, and later, all the contestants attended a dinner hosted in Jurys Hotel, College Green, Dublin, by Ferguson Tractors. In the National Championships that year, women were admitted for the first time, listed in the "Farmerette Class", and the winner was crowned "Queen of the Plough".

The first Irish Sheep Shearing Championship (hand and machine) was held in the Navan Showgrounds (Co Meath) in June, organised by Macra na Feirme, and was won by T. Bourke of Ballymore Eustace, County Wicklow.

The 3-day Summer Show in Ballintemple, Cork, was held at the Munster Agricultural Society Showgrounds on Monaghans Road. In July, the Kildare County Show was held in Athy, and also the Leix County Show in Rathdowney (County Laois). In August, the 2-day Galway Horse Show (showjumping) was held, and likewise the Limerick Show (showjumping), the latter including a Dog Show and Agricultural Show.

Flooding

The Irish Times had an article once a month called "The Sky in January" or whatever month was being discussed, authored by either Armagh Observatory (Northern Ireland) or Dunsink Observatory (north county Dublin). There would be an egg-shaped sketch of the sky, with the important stars marked. 1952 and 1953 were exceptionally dry, whereas 1954 was very wet. Dr E. M Lindsay of Armagh reported in January 1955: "Records show that for centuries past there have been cycles of abnormal conditions and we can expect more in the future. Indeed we might say that our weather would be truly abnormal if there were no abnormalities." Earthquakes were also a feature of 1953 and 1954, e.g. central Europe, and central Algeria (Oceanville).

There was serious flooding in Ireland in October, 1954, especially in the River Shannon basin (catchment area). The River Nore also burst its banks, leading to flooding in John Street in Kilkenny. More bad flooding occurred in December in the River Shannon catchment area, apparently the worst since 1880, and boats had to be used for rescue purposes. To cap it all, there was very heavy snow at the end of January, especially in Galway/Mayo.

Arising from a poor Summer, and the Autumn floods, the unsaved crops caused much anxiety amongst the farming community.

In November, the Army helped farmers to save hay (obviously very late at this stage). Schoolchildren, and 40 soldiers from Griffith Barracks and Cathal Brugha Barracks in Dublin, helped farmers in Rathfarnham and Blanchardstown to bring in the harvest (potatoes and wheat). In October, wheat was fetching 75s to 82s 6d a barrel. The late harvest and high moisture content of the wheat was putting pressure on the kilns in the flour mills. Grain lorries had to queue overnight for warehouse space on East Wall Road in Dublin.

Industry

<u>Building Products</u>

Clarecastle Clay Products, in County Clare, which made land drainage pipes, opened a new £97,000 factory, which was blessed by the Bishop of Killaloe, and dedicated to Our Lady, with a statue erected over the entrance.
     Cement Ltd in Drogheda erected a 170 foot high steel chimney, made by Universal Fabricators in Finglas.

<u>Clothing</u>

A workers strike (who ever heard of a management strike!) in Edward Donaghy & Sons in Drogheda, who made shoes, lasted a few months.
     Sunbeam Wolsey was a big employer in Millfield, County Cork (founded 1928), and was engaged in spinning and weaving of woollen textiles, hosiery, etc, with a subsidiary called Middleton Worsted Mills.
     Connaught Cosiwear (hosiery factory founded in 1932) on the North Mall in Westport, was rebuilt in 1954, after a fire in 1953.

<u>Food</u>

Another Ranks Flour wheat grain silo was completed in Limerick city in November, supplementing the three existing grain silos. The new one held 15,000 tons, was 144 ft high, 150 ft long, and 66 ft wide, with eight large and three small bins, all hexagonal. Collen Bros was the contractor for the reinforced concrete structure, which was completed in eight months, assisted by an electric crane. The English company, Joseph Rank Ltd, had taken over the existing Goodbody Flour mill in 1930, and were building new grain storage silos and dryers on the Dock Road, over a long period of time. The premises closed in 1983.

Cleeves Toffee Bars were made by the Condensed Milk Company, founded in Limerick in 1889, but the company was more famous for its tins of condensed milk.

In January, a new factory was opened by Sean Lemass (Minister for Industry & Commerce) in Ballinasloe, County Galway, for Burnhouse Ireland Ltd, farm feeds, fertilisers and animal oils, and was also blessed by the Parish Priest.

"Bacon factories received about 40,000 pigs last week" read the headline in one of the national newspapers, good news for lovers of rashers and sausages, or bacon and cabbage.

Electricity

1954 saw the opening of the ESB's "Marina" power station in Cork Docks, on the south bank of the River Lee, near the Ford car assembly plant, Dunlops rubber tyre factory, the Cork Milling Company, and the National Flour Mills. The new power station ran on both coal and oil. In Co Offaly, the Ferbane milled-peat electricity power station was in the course of construction during 1954, including the two 270-feet (80 metres) high cooling towers, but the station was demolished in 2003. Allenwood Power Station (peat-fired) opened in County Kildare in 1952, but was demolished in 1994.

In 1954, the first delivery of bulk oil arrived at Lapps Quay in Cork, having been imported by Tedcastle McCormick in the tanker "Flisvos" from the Coryton Refinery on the River Thames near London.

Quarries & Mines

Bord na Mona, the State company which exploited the turf bogs in the midlands, supplied milled peat to some electricity power stations, and also manufactured Peat Briquettes for domestic use, especially for flat-dwellers and bedsitting rooms. The company was advertising in May for 1,000 workers, for five midland sites, at wages of 2/- per hour, for a 48-hour week.

Silvermines is a village near Nenagh in County Tipperary, made famous for its lead and zinc mines, which had re-opened in 1949.

Weatherall of Clondalkin, Co Dublin, makers of plasterboard, concrete pipes and concrete roof tiles, bought the disused Greenore Port in County Louth, including the railway station cum hotel, from British Railways. They already had a gypsum quarry in nearby Kingscourt in County Cavan, and intended to build a gypsum plaster factory in Greenore, although this never came to fruition.

Miscellaneous

The famous producer, John Huston, was making the film "Moby Dick" in Youghal, County Cork, in July, using the sailing schooner "Pequod".

Glass cutters and engravers were being educated in Waterford Technical School, in preparation for a good job in Waterford Crystal Company, which had been opened in 1947 by experts from Prague in Czechoslovakia.

In 1954, there was a fire in Irish Tanners, Portlaw, Co Waterford, which was in the business of making leather from cattle hides, in the period from 1935 to 1985. Their site was the former Malcolmson spinning and weaving cotton factory, a notable Quaker enterprise in the 19th century.

Tourism

The Tostal cultural festival was not just confined to Dublin, and there were parades and other events in the big cities and towns around Ireland. At Easter, there was a big Patrician Pageant (in honour of St Patrick, patron saint of Ireland), in the Boyne Valley, based around the Hill of Tara, and the Viaduct Field in Drogheda, and included a Pascal Fire in Slane in front of Lord Mountcharles's castle.

In January, 1954, a site was selected for Cork Airport at Ballygarvan, and the airport opened in 1961.

Shannon Airport had been in existence since the 1930's, and the famous Shannon School of Hotel Training was founded in 1951.

In 1954, Lord Gort bought the ruined Bunratty Castle, which included two chapels, and he then rebuilt it, with assistance from the Office of Public Works, and opened it to the public six years later.

Ilnacullin, with its Italian gardens, also known as Garnish Island, off Glengariff in County Cork, was bequeathed to the State in 1954 by Roland L'Estrange Bryce.

The 4th Wexford Festival of Music & Art took place over 8 days, starting on the 31st Oct, opening with the opera "La Sonnambula". This later became the Wexford Opera Festival, and is still a popular annual cultural event.

Butlins Holiday Camp, Mosney, County Meath, opened in 1949, and was popular with Irish tourists, and even day-trippers. The bedrooms were in small individual chalets (and not tents), and the floor staff wore lovely red jackets and white trousers. Meals were provided in the large cafeteria, and evening entertainment took place in a big hall, featuring cabaret artists, such as the comedian, Jack Cruise in July. The Irish Independent newspaper organised a weekend outing for 200 staff during the Summer, such was the glamour of the camp. Normally, the big companies only provided a day-outing for staff to various locations around Ireland, usually using trains or hired buses. The former holiday camp closed in recent decades, and for the past ten years has been a "Direct Provision" centre for foreign asylum seekers, a type of open-air prison.

In April, there was a residential course in the Hodson Bay Hotel, Athlone, for foremen and supervisors, organised by the School of Commerce, Rathmines, Dublin.

The Vale View Hotel (Moores), in the Vale of Avoca, County Wicklow, was closed for the Winter, from 1st October until the following Easter.

Newspaper headlines during 1954 included "Westport Plans to Attract Tourists" (County Mayo), and "Good Trout Fishing in Poulaphouca" (County Wicklow).

Sport

Besides the big racecourses in and around Dublin, horse-racing on a smaller scale was popular in such places as Navan in June, Tramore in Waterford in August, and even on the beach at Laytown Strand, Co Meath.

In March there was a meeting of the Wicklow Harriers (Stag Hunt Meet) outside Gorey in County Wexford, where a crowd of spectators followed them around the course. The national newspapers had a photo of the Waterford Beagles on their opening meet of their hunt, at Half Way House, Waterford.

The October, the national newspapers included articles about the pheasant season.

The Wakefield Trophy Car Race took place at the Curragh in County Kildare in August.

In April, the Irish Open Fencing Championship was held in Cork.

Social

"The Ballroom of Romance", a short story by William Trevor, gives a good idea of night-life in remoter parts of Ireland in 1954. There were hundreds of Ballrooms (Dance Halls), and dozens of roving dance-bands, the latter similar to a small orchestra, although there were also some ceili bands in rural areas. The more glamorous and lively Showbands only appeared in the 1960's.

In February, the New Astoria Ballroom opened in Bundoran, County Donegal, with Chick Smith & His Orchestra.

The famous "Fleadh Cheoil" started in Mullingar in 1951, as did Comhaltas Ceoltoiri Eireann, and in August 1954 the Fleadh took place in Cavan (and came back in 2010, 2011, and 2012).

Other festivals included the second Meath Drama Festival in March in Navan CYMS Hall, the Sligo Feis Ceoil in April, the All-Ireland Amateur Drama Festival (two weeks in May), Ardee Carnival (18th June to 4th July), and the Tostal "Bridge International" in Galway.

Mrs Lawlors hotel in Naas held a St Stephens Night Gala Dinner Dance.

In 1954, President Kelly opened An Grianan (residential college) in Termonfeckin, Co Louth, for the Irish Countrywomens Association (ICA). The property was a gift from the Kellogg Foundation in America (corn-flakes), and was previously the Tearnan Hotel.

Miscellaneous

In June, there was a photo in the Irish Independent newspaper of the 1st Motor Squadron team, winners of the Gustav Submachine-Gun Competition at the Southern Command Army Shooting Competition in Kilworth Camp, Co Cork. There was also a photo of the Army in Gormanston Camp (Barracks), Couth Meath, practicing with anti-aircraft guns – did nobody tell them that the War was over? The Summer also heralded Army Week in the Curragh Training Camp, with shooting competitions. Another June photo was of the newly formed Irish Naval Service Choir, Haulbowline, Cobh, on their official visit to Mount Melleray Abbey, Cappoquin, Co Waterford. There was a big Pioneer rally in Killarney in June, promoting abstinence from alcohol, but no doubt the army lads were too busy to attend.

The building of the Galway Regional Hospital started in 1950, and partly opened in March 1954.

In January, a new single-storey clinic opened in Tullamore, County Offaly, replacing the existing dispensary. The building of a new Nurses Home for the Hospital also commenced.

The building of the Medical Missionaries of Mary hospital started in Drogheda in 1953, and was expected to be finished in phases by September 1957, at a cost of £500,000. In November 1954, the Pope donated £10,000 of his own money to the nun's project.

In anticipation of telephones becoming popular, the Department of Posts and Telegraphs dug a trench (by mechanical digger) across the width of Ireland for an underground telephone cable.

Fifty-four new Council houses opened in Kells, County Meath, on the Moynalty Road, at a total cost of £82,000, and in celebration there was a parade through the town, and then dinner for the local dignitaries in the Headford Arms Hotel.

In August, there was the Annual Gift Day at the Protestant Girls Orphanage in Greystones, Co Wicklow (Kimberly, La Touche Road). Miss Adeline Mathers was the motherly matron, having started her time as a young lady when the orphanage was in Harold's Cross, Dublin, beside Healys Grocery Shop in the village centre.

There were frequent photos in the Irish Independent newspaper, often aerial, of different towns around the country. One such photo in January was of Keem Bay on the west side of Achill Island (off Mayo), showing some fishermen looking for basking sharks.

Articles in the national newspapers of interest to rural readers included such headlines as: "Light Sussex Chickens", "How a water diviner works with a forked sally rod", "List of Country Fairs", and "Onion Industry in West Kerry".

Rural Ireland would not be complete without some itinerant tinsmiths (gypsies) in colourful horse-drawn barrel-vaulted caravans, mending pots and pans for farmers, in exchange for a few free-range eggs, a loaf of home-made soda bread, and a jug of steaming fresh milk. Nowadays their descendants are called travellers (not to be confused with commercial travellers or salesmen of a bygone era), and tend to reside more comfortably in suburban areas, engaged in roof repairs and tarmac driveways.

Knock Apparition Chapel on left, and old church on right.

162

Knock Apparition Chapel as it was from 1940 to 1979. (Courtesy of Knock Museum).

Current view of Knock Apparition Chapel.

Above and below: Butlins/Mosney Holiday Camp is now a "Direct Provision Centre" for foreign Asylum Seekers, a type of long-term "open-prison".

World Affairs

Britain

Most of the 1950's was a hard time for jobs in rural Ireland, forcing thousands of young people to emigrate, especially to England, where, because of extensive bomb-damage, there was a post-war building boom, especially in housing, and also a demand for good nurses to operate the new National Health Service. World War Two rationing in England, especially meat, ended on 4th July, 1954, making daily life easier.

In January, 1954, Britain closed its Labour Liaison Office in Dublin, which had been set up during World War Two to organise Irish workers crossing over to England, matching the specific needs of the British "war effort" (such as factories making guns, bullets, shells, tanks, aircraft, etc). Dublin women already had experience of making "shells" during the First World War in a factory at 43 Parkgate Street, on the bank of the River Liffey beside Heuston Bridge, which was later occupied by Cahill Printers, and in recent decades by Hickey Fabrics.

In London, the Galtymore Ballroom (opened in 1952) at 94 Cricklewood Broadway, near Kilburn, was a mecca for Irish people seeking romance and all the home news.

The Catholic Church kept an eye on Irish immigrants in England, and at one point during the Marian year of 1954, the Tricolour (Irish flag of green white and orange) flew over Wembley Stadium, London, when Cardinal Griffin placed a precious gold crown on a statue of "Our Lady of Willesden" (named after an Irish area near Kilburn).

The Irish actress, Siobhan McKenna, was given good reviews in the London newspapers for her title role in "St Joan", a play by George Bernard Shaw, running at the London Arts Theatre in 1954.

Famous Irish golfer, Christy O'Connor, fell at the last green in the "News of the World" sponsored Championship Tournament in St Andrews, Scotland.

Surprisingly, in 1954, there was a plea in the House of Commons by Belfast MPs for the return of some Hugh Lane paintings (continental artists) to Ireland, and five years later there was an agreement to share the art treasures on a rotating basis every five years, between the National Gallery in London, and the National Gallery in Dublin. Hugh Lane, a rich art dealer of Irish descent, had set up the Municipal Gallery of Modern Art in Dublin in 1908, which is now housed in Parnell Square, but following his untimely death in 1915, there was a dispute over the bequest of other paintings to London instead of Dublin, as stipulated in a codicil (unfortunately not witnessed) to his will.

The 25-year old Queen Elizabeth II was officially crowned on the 2nd June 1953 in Westminster Abbey in London. She had actually succeeded to the position on the 6th February, 1952, following the death of her father, King George VI. She had already married Prince Philip, on the 20th November 1947, who was born in Greece, and was actually a Prince of both Greece and Denmark, but changed his name to Mountbatten when he became a naturalised British citizen just before the marriage. Following her coronation, she and her entourage completed a 50,000 mile world tour of her Commonwealth subjects, from November 1953 to May 1954. She managed to visit Belfast in August 1954, to launch the "Southern Cross" ship. The royal yacht "Britannia" had completed her maiden voyage to Malta in April 1954.

Winston Churchill celebrated his 80th birthday on the 30th November 1954, and in 1955 he resigned as leader of the Conservative Political Party, and was replaced by Anthony Eden.

The London Motor Show was held in Earls Court Exhibition Centre at the end of October, with Czechoslovakia (behind the Iron Curtain) sending a Skoda car and station-wagon for exhibition. In December, the Smithfield Show took place in the same venue, for livestock and farm machinery.

"Hancocks Half Hour" of comedy sketches started on BBC radio in November, 1954, and the television version of George Orwell's novel, "Nineteen Eighty Four", was screened on the BBC that same year. The "Guinness Book of Records" was launched in 1955 in England, and is today a world-wide annual best-seller.

On 6th May, 1954, Roger Bannister, a medical student, ran the mile in Oxford in 3 minutes 59 seconds, a world record. On 29th May, Diane Leather ran the mile in under 5-minutes in Birmingham.

In January, the collier Wallace Rose, which was often in Dublin, sank in the Thames Estuary (Erith head) after colliding with the bigger merchant ship Yvonne, with the death of nine sailors and two survivors.

During 1954, there was a major dockers strike in Britain, crippling imports and exports, which ended on the 2nd November.

There was a terrible fog (smog) in London for a week in December 1952, which killed around 12,000 people, mostly old, and caused serious illness in many more people.

Colonies

Following the Second World War, which relied heavily on American men, machinery and big dollar loans, Britain (and other colonists) had no option but to abandon their lucrative colonies, and many countries demanded their Independence. India achieved its freedom in 1947, although before the British abandoned ship, they drew a hasty line on the map, and declared that the top section was to be re-named Pakistan, for Muslim occupation only, resulting in a terrible civil war throughout the sub-continent.

"Malayan Rubber in Jeopardy" ran an Irish newspaper headline in October 1954. An enquiry by the British colonists noted with concern the research into synthetic rubber being carried out by scientists in Europe and America. Half of the rubber trees in Malaya (60,000 acres in total), which produced natural white rubber syrup, were over 30 years old. The British moaned about the high cost of fighting Malayan "terrorists" (in reality, fully justified Native freedom-fighters), including the cost of erecting barbed-wire fences, new workers housing, transport of resettled labour etc, which placed a heavy burden on planters. Within a few years, Malaya was Independent.

Since 1952, the Mau Mau in Kenya had rebelled against British colonists, which was met by savage British Army reprisals, appalling concentration camps, etc, but Independence was finally won in 1963.

The British colony of Nigeria becomes independent in October 1960, after nearly one hundred years of occupation. Cyprus, another British colony, also achieved Independence in 1960.

Following the First World War, the British and French colonised parts of the former Ottoman Empire in the Middle-East, with the British occupying Iraq (originally called Mesopotamia) and Palestine, and the French occupying Syria and Lebanon. Even before this war, Jewish Zionists from all over the world had been flooding Arab Palestine, as a way of occupation by stealth, and after the First World War, the British encouraged this subversive activity, by virtue of the Balfour Declaration. After the turmoil of the Second World War, the Zionists seized their opportunity, kicked the British out, killed or drove most of the remaining native Palestinians into neighbouring countries, and declared themselves owners of Arab Palestine, renaming the country as Israel. Not surprisingly, the few remaining Palestinians are still fighting in 2021 for the return of their land, despite being forcibly restricted to concentration-camp-style areas such as the Gaza Strip and the West Bank. In 1954, the new Jewish state of Israel (in reality, Arabic Palestine under foreign Jewish occupation) bought 3,000 tons of seed potatoes from the gullible Irish, and nowadays, Israel exports its potatoes to the lazy and irresponsible Irish!

The oil-fields of Iran (originally called Persia) were the cause of many international disputes. Mr Mossadegh, the Prime Minister of Iran, had nationalised the Anglo-Iranian Oil Company in 1950, and became an ally of the Soviet Union. In 1953, the UK and USA helped to organise a coup d'état against Mossadegh, allowing the Shah of Iran to return from exile. Hence, the Anglo-Persian Oil Company dispute was settled in August 1954, allowing an American consortium to manage the oil fields, and buy oil from Iran in the future, after paying £25 million compensation.

Although Egypt nominally achieved Independence in 1922, the British remained in occupation especially around the Suez Canal. In 1956, Egypt nationalised the Suez Canal, and after a few months of war against Egypt by the British, with the collusion of Israel and France, the

168

Americans interceded diplomatically on behalf of Egypt, with threats to ruin the British financial system, which had the desired effect, and a huge embarrassment to the deflated British. However, the British evacuation of the Suez Canal zone had already started before this war, and there was a photo in the Irish Independent in August, 1954, showing British soldiers of the Parachute Regiment boarding the troopship, "Empire Ken", in Port Said, on the way back to their motherland.

Mr Theodore Pike from Cashel in County Tipperary left Dublin in January 1954 to take up his new post of Governor General of British Somaliland in East Africa. He was previously senior provincial commissioner in Tanganyika. Pike had played rugby for Ireland in 1927/28. His younger brother, Rev Victor Pike, was in 1954 the Chaplain General of the British Forces. These appointments and many more, show how some Irish people (not doubt of Protestant stock) were British overseas colonists, while the rest of Ireland was struggling over hundreds of years for independence from British occupation.

Europe

Pope Pius X was canonised a saint in St Peter's Basilica, Rome, on the 29th May, 1954, in front of a huge crowd. Five other saints were canonised that same year in Rome.

Ireland's chapel in the crypt of St Peters Basilica, Rome, was dedicated on 11th September, and could accommodate forty people. This event was organised by the Knights of St Columbanus in Dublin.

In October, a Marian Year Congress was held at Fatima, including a Pontifical Mass at the Chapel of Apparitions, presided over by Pope Pius XII, and on the 8th December, the Pope officially closed the Marian Year from his sick bed (he recovered later).

There was a big ceremony in Rome on the 1st November, when the Pope instituted the Feast of Queenship of Mary (Regina caeli), with the annual feast-day now on the 31st May.

Over 20,000 Irish pilgrims visited Lourdes in France throughout 1954 (Grotto of Massabielle). The affluent flew by Aer Lingus, but the majority went by trains and ships to Paris, then a 13-hour train trip to the Grotto. In August, the Dublin Diocesan Pilgrimage made the trip, with Archbishop McQuaid flying.

During the year, there was a photo in the Irish newspapers of the Irish team in the General Franco "March-Past" at the Athletic Championships held by the International Federation of the Society of Catholic Students at San Sebastian (Spain). On another occasion, there was an Irish Press photo of General MacEoin, Minister for Defence in Ireland, chatting with General Franco in El Prado Palace, Madrid.

Throughout the year, the Nine-Power Talks made progress, in relation to Germany and Italy after the Second World War, and the ending of the Allied Occupation, resulting in the Brussels Treaty. Irish exports to West Germany had started in 1953, and in January, 1954, the Irish Army Show-Jumping team attended competitions in Berlin. East and West Germany were re-united in 1989 after the "fall" of the Berlin wall.

In the field of sport, the Union of European Football Associations (UEFA) was set up in Basel in Switzerland in 1954. That same year, West Germany beat Hungary, 3-2, winning the FIFA World Cup, in Bern, Switzerland. On November 13th 1954, England beat France in Paris (30,000 crowd) in the first Rugby League World Cup.

Far East

The Korean War ended in 1953 after more than 3 years, splitting the country on a north-south divide, and the buffer zone is still in place.

The Geneva Agreement in July 1954 marked the end of the 1st Indochina War (1st Vietnam War) ousting the French colonists. The country was divided, leaving Communists in the north half, supported by the Soviet Union, prompting America to declare war in November 1955, and the start of the 2nd Vietnam War.

In May 1953, a British expedition reached the top of Mount Everest, but the first person in the team was New Zealander, Edmund Hillary, and his native Sherpa, Tenzing Norgay.

Africa

1954 saw the start of the Algerian War of Independence against French colonists, which struggle lasted eight years.

USSR/Russia

Joseph Stalin died in 1953, aged 73, and Nikita Khrushchev became the new leader.

In 1954, the Crimea region was transferred from Russia to the Ukraine, but in 2014, was annexed back by Russia.

The world's first Atomic Power Station opened near Moscow (Obninsk) in 1954.

The USSR developed its own Hydrogen-bomb in 1953, which was superior to the one made by America in 1952, and this triggered the start of the "Arms Race" between the two super-powers.

America

The Irish who emigrated to America did far better than those who went to England, because roots had been set down from the Famine period of the 1840's. In 1954, the Ellis Island Immigration Station, beside the Statue of Liberty in New York Harbour, closed. Annie Moore, a 15-year old Irish girl, was the first to be processed in 1892.

"The Nautilus", the world's first nuclear-powered submarine, was delivered to the US Navy. The prototype for the Boeing 707, Americas first jet airplane, was launched in 1954.

On the 8th April, 1954, two Canadian airplanes collided in mid-air in Saskatchewan, killing 37 people. The small Royal Canadian Air Force training plane, with only the 22-year old trainee pilot on board, crashed into a commercial plane (31 passengers and 4 crew), and part of the debris from the crash landed on a house, killing the occupant.

Hurricane Hazel hit the Caribbean on 14th/15th October, killing at least 1,000 in Haiti. This region has been prone to earthquakes, flooding and hurricanes for at least the past two hundred years.

1954 witnessed pioneering events in America in the field of medicine, such as the first human trials of "the contraceptive pill" for women, and the first kidney transplant in Boston. Jonas Salk's polio vaccine was trialed in 1954 on 1.3m children, and then licenced in 1955. In 1953, while doing research in England, Crick (English) and Watson (American) published their famous paper on the double-helix nature of DNA.

The Rock 'n Roll era started in April 1954, when Bill Haley & The Comets released "Rock Around the Clock". In July, Elvis Presley released "That's All Right". Heart-stopper actress Marilyn Monroe married Joe DeMaggio, baseball star, in San Francisco City Hall. RCA introduced the first colour television set in America. "Playboy" men-only magazine started in December 1953. Burger King opened in Miami, Florida, in December, and McDonalds opened in 1955, both heralding in the "fast-food" era, which is still with us. Disneyland opened in California in 1955.

Senator Joseph McCarty of Wisconsin was censured by the Senate, 67 to 22, thus ending his maverick witch-hunt against alleged Communists. He died three years later.

US President, Dwight D. Eisenhower, authorised the Central Intelligence Agency (CIA) to support the military coup in Guatemala, starting a decades-long Civil War.

In 1954, there was a riot in Baltimore, in protest against negro children attending white schools. That same year, the Supreme Court had ruled that segregation of whites and blacks in schools violated the Constitution. Martin Luther King (Junior) became active in 1955, and went on to make his famous speech in Washington in August 1963, "I have a dream", at a time when the infamous Ku Klux Klan was very active.

In June, 1954, Rocky Marciano, 29 year old world heavyweight boxing champion, retained his title in New York against Ezzard Chaires, former champion, winning on points over 15 rounds.

Tourist Board map of Dublin in the 1950's.

Printed in Great Britain
by Amazon